upper-intermediate

TARGET!

Akira Morita   Makiko Iio   Takehiro Hashimoto

Mari Kakuta   Mai Satake   Taron Plaza

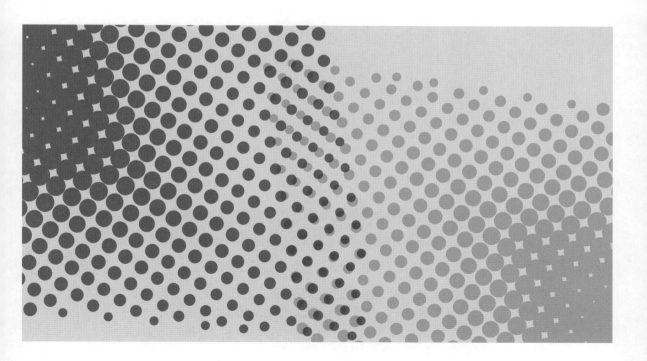

KINSEIDO

Kinseido Publishing Co., Ltd.

3-21 Kanda Jimbo-cho, Chiyoda-ku,
Tokyo 101-0051, Japan

First published 2021 by Kinseido Publishing Co., Ltd.

Cover design sein
Text design   Yasuharu Yuki
Illustrations   Toru Igarashi

音声ファイル無料ダウンロード

http://www.kinsei-do.co.jp/download/4118

この教科書で ⬇ DL 00 の表示がある箇所の音声は、上記 URL または QR コードにて
無料でダウンロードできます。自習用音声としてご活用ください。

▶ PC からのダウンロードをお勧めします。スマートフォンなどでダウンロードされる場合は、
　ダウンロード前に「解凍アプリ」をインストールしてください。
▶ URL は、検索ボックスではなくアドレスバー(URL 表示欄)に入力してください。
▶ お使いのネットワーク環境によっては、ダウンロードできない場合があります。

◉ CD 00　左記の表示がある箇所の音声は、教室用 CD (Class Audio CD) に収録されています。

は　し　が　き

　TARGET! は、聞く、読むから話す、書くへと繋がるタスクを進めながら、言語の 4 技能を無理なく学習できるグレード別の総合教材シリーズです。

　この *upper-intermediate*（準上級）レベルでは、基礎を定着させ、その英語力をより様々な状況で運用できるレベルにまで伸ばすことを目標としています。

　書名が示すように、各課で目標となる TARGET! を明示しています。これによって学習者諸君は、これから学ぶことだけでなく、自分の学習を振り返ることができるでしょう。LISTENING セクションでは、聞き取りに必要なポイントやコツを整理し、身近なトピックによる会話でその応用を学びます。これが、自信を持てる発話に繋がるわけです。READING セクションでは文法項目の基本を整理しながら、課全体のテーマによる、まとまりのある文章（500 語程度）から文章の展開法、英語の論理構成も学びます。ここから、効率良く、かつ正確に自らの考えを伝えられる発話とライティングが可能になります。

　以下は、本書のタスクを行う上でのヒントです。クラスでの活動に活かしてください。

大項目	中項目	タスク	ねらいと学習法
LISTENING	Listening	**TARGET!**	英語の発音の特徴を理解し、日本語話者にとって聞き取りのポイントとなる点を整理して学びます。さらに、発音に留まらず、英文を聞いて理解するポイントについても機能的側面から学びます。
		WARM UP	TARGET! の確認を行うタスクです。スペリングに注意することも大切です。
		TRY LISTENING	応用部分です。やや聞き取りにくい、ここが聞き取れれば、まるで違う、というポイントも含まれているので、聞き取りの後、発音の練習もしてみましょう。クイズ感覚で楽しむことができます。
	Listening & Speaking	**CONVERSATION**	「発音と聞き取りのテーマ」に基づいた会話の聞き取りです。 A では、それまでに学んだ聞き取りのポイントを、場面に当てはめて聞き取れるか確認します。その後は 2 つの設問を聞いて会話の内容を理解しているかどうかを試します。 B では、聞き取りの確認、そしてそれ以外の部分の発音も確認しながら、ペア学習を行います。お互いに気づいた点があったら、臆せず指摘し合いましょう。棒読みにならないよう、気持ちの動きにも注目して読みましょう。 C では、指示に従って、新たに会話を作ってみましょう。学んでいる TARGET! を最後まで意識してください。
READING	Reading & Grammar	**SHORT ANNOUNCEMENT**	ここでは、様々な場面で耳にするアナウンスメントを実践的に学びます。あるまとまった情報をキャッチすることは、聞き取りが必要になるもう一つの重要な状況です。 A は聞き取りの問題です。事前にざっと読んで下線部を予測してみる学習法もあります。 B は、内容確認です。どこで語っていた情報か確認しましょう。 C では、アナウンスメント部分を十分に活用しながら、少し違ったシチュエーションも含め、自分（たち）のオリジナルなアナウンスメントを作ってみましょう。クラスメイトと協力するのも良いことです。

READING	**Reading & Grammar**	**TARGET!**	文法のおさらいです。基本事項をしっかり押さえておけば、英文の「ルール」自体は、それほど難しいものではありません。例外より、基本が何かに注目しましょう。
		GRAMMAR EXERCISE 1, 2	TARGET! の確認です。他にも自分で思いつくもの（問題）がないか、積極的に考えてみましょう。
		DEFINITION FOR READING	英語の感覚をつかむためには、英語で理解することが大切です。英単語を日本語を介さずに理解してみましょう。Computer を「電子計算機」とか「電脳」と訳してもピンときませんね。
		READING	しっかりと情報を理解するためには、ある程度の長さが必要です。だらだら長いのではなく、（実用的）文章には構造があります。いくつかの課を終えたら、構造の共通点を話し合ってみましょう。間違えていてもよいので、未知の単語や表現は、辞書で調べておきましょう。学んだ文法項目の整理もします。
		COMPREHENSION	READING の各部分の理解が適切であったかを確認します。全体として言いたいこと（main idea）と、その理解のための（具体）例やデータをきちんと切り分けましょう。
	Writing & Grammar	**MAKE A SUMMARY**	COMPREHENSION も活用し、summary を作ります。復習も兼ね、重要な表現も学びます。完成させたあと、模範解答を確認し、それをもう一度音声だけで聞いてみるのも良い学習法です。明快な文章は明快な summary になります。あまり難しく考えないでやってみましょう。
	Integration	**HAVE YOUR SAY**	文章全体の構成（構造）を意識し、自分の writing、まとまりを持った paragraph writing ができるようになるための task です。お互いの文を比べることによって、文章の構成について、反省し学ぶことも多いはずです。文章の一貫性と、文の順番（文章構成）に注意しましょう。

　教科書の設問は、試験問題ではありません。学生諸君の理解を助けるための道しるべ、そして理解の確認をするための道具です。うまく聞き取れなかったら、そこは、確認が必要な部分だ、ということですから、もう一度聞いてみましょう。もし、それでもまだ聞き取れなかったら、まずは聞こえた音を丸ごと、その部分の発音のイメージとしてみましょう。READING 部分は、タイトルを参考にしながら、全体として言いたいことをはっきりさせましょう。本文中に、明示されている場合もありますから、これだ！という文を見つけてみましょう。これを main idea と呼びますが、この main idea の理解を助けるための具体例やデータに注目しすぎないようにして読みましょう。

　最後に、本シリーズは3レベルでの構成を考えていましたが、好評を得て、この4つ目のレベルの出版をすることができました。シリーズを通して、金星堂の代表取締役社長福岡正人さん、編集部 長島吉成さんと蔦原美智さんには、大変お世話になりました。特に、長島さんには企画から細かい作業まで、出版の全ての作業にわたってお世話になりました。この場を借りて、厚く御礼申し上げます。

著者一同

Table of Contents

Life with Pets

ペットとともに生きる

LISTENING

音の連結・同化を聞き取りましょう　　🎧 DL 02　💿 CD1-02

1. 連結＝隣り合う音（子音＋母音）がつながること

/l/, /r/＋母音	a handful of your eyes
/f/, /v/, /s/, /z/, /sh/＋母音	laugh at give up pass away hundreds of brush up
/m/, /n/＋母音	come in in addition
/p/, /t/, /d/, /k/, /g/, /ch/ ＋母音	drop out a lot of find out check in dig out watch out

2. 同化＝隣り合う音がつながり、音が変化すること

/t/, /ts/ + /y/	last year Nice to meet you. She lets your children join.
/d/, /dz/ + /y/	Did you... ? Could you... ? She needs your help.
/s/, /z/ + /y/	this year bless you Does your mother know her?

WARM UP　　🎧 DL 03　💿 CD1-03

１〜５の文を聞いて、音が連結・同化している箇所に下線を引いてみましょう。

1. Please take apples and oranges as you want. They are good.

2. Is it possible to keep up with practicing baseball in this cold weather?

3. I found hundreds of seashells on the beach.

4. That shirt suits you! I bet you like it.

5. She always makes you smile.

TRY LISTENING　　🎧 DL 04　💿 CD1-04

次の文を聞いて、（　　）に入る部分を補って文を完成させましょう。

My name is Yuka. (　　　　　) (　　　　　) (　　　　　) (　　　　　) student.
I'll (　　　　　) (　　　　) to my family. We are (　　　　　) (　　　　　)
(　　　　　) my father, mother, brother and me. My father (　　　　　　)
(　　　) an IT company. My mother is a (　　　　) (　　　　　). And my brother is
now (　　　　　) (　　　　　) to (　　　　) (　　　　) economics.

CONVERSATION

🎧 DL 05   💿 CD1-05

A. 次の会話を聞き、下線部に適切な語句を入れましょう。会話のあとに問題が流れるので、適切な答えを a、b から選びましょう。

Three students are talking about an upcoming trip.

Paul: Hi, guys. Getting ready for your trip to Malaysia?

Erina: We sure are, but there is still so much to pack!

Eddy: By the way, Paul, we were hoping we could
¹_____ while we are away.

Paul: Sure, what is it?

Erina: We were wondering if ²_____
_____, Toby and Jody. You would just
need to stop by once a day and check their
food and water.

Eddy: We thought about putting them in a boarding kennel but it would put
us at ease if we knew they were in their own home.

Paul: I'd be happy to do it. I love dogs, so it will be fun.

Erina: Thank you so much! ³_____!

Eddy: We'll make sure ⁴_____ some nice souvenirs!

Paul: It's ⁵_____. In fact, I'm looking forward to it!

Q1. **a.** They were worrying about how to take care of their dogs while they were away.
b. They were worrying about the expense of a boarding kennel for their dogs.

Q2. **a.** They came up with a good Malaysian souvenir for Paul.
b. They thought it was a big help for them.

B. クラスメートとペアを組み、完成した会話を発話練習してみましょう。

C. ▨ 部を参考に、同じペアで次の①または②のシチュエーションで会話をしてみましょう。

① 研修旅行（study tour）で留守の間、小鳥（bird, parrot, etc.）の世話を頼む。

② 犬の散歩のアルバイト（a part-time job as a dog-walker, a dog walking job）を一緒に手伝ってくれないかと頼む。

SHORT ANNOUNCEMENT

A. 次の宣伝メッセージを聞き、下線部に適切な語句を入れましょう。

Are you planning a trip out of town? Do you have ¹ _____ _____ during your trip? If so, we at the Airport Pet Hotel are here for you. We are located right in the airport and have all the necessary facilities to ensure that your pet has a stress free and comfortable stay ² _____. You can choose between a private room for your pet or a shared space with other animals. Additionally, we have an open space for your pet to run and play freely without a leash. Trimming services are also available during your pet's stay. We happily accept dogs, cats and other small animals; however we cannot accommodate fish or exceptionally large animals. For reservations and inquiries, please call the Airport Pet Hotel at 03-7218-6556. ³ _____,

knowing your pet is being well taken care of!

B. 次の文がメッセージの内容に合致している場合は T、そうでない場合は F を選択しましょう。

1. The shop offers a trimming service before pets and owners take a trip.

[T / F]

2. The shop is located in the airport facilities. [T / F]

3. In a private room, pets can play without a leash on. [T / F]

C. ペアを組み、　　部を参考に次のようなホテルの特徴をアナウンスしてみましょう。必要に応じて自分たちで情報を付け加えて話しましょう。

- 洋式の部屋（a Western style room）か和式の部屋を選ぶことができます。
- 予約なしの（without reservation）お客や、宿泊の延長（extension of stay）も喜んで受け付けます。

4

READING

TARGET!

基本的な文の種類を学びましょう

文の意味によっていくつかの種類に分かれます。

[基本的な文]

平叙文　事実や考えをありのまま述べる文

　（肯定文）She owns a huge house. ／（否定文）I can't run so fast.

疑問文　質問する文。文末に？（クエスチョンマーク）をつける

　Are you Mr. Bettis?　　When did you go to Canada?

[特殊な文]

命令文　「～しなさい」と相手に命令する文。please をつけると依頼にもなる

　Open the window. ／ Don't speak Japanese here.（命令）

　Pass me the soy sauce, please.（依頼）

感嘆文　おどろき、喜び、悲しみなどの感情を強く表す文。文末に！をつける

　What a wonderful day it is! ／ How cute she is!

GRAMMAR EXERCISE 1

日本語を参考に［　　　］内の語句を並べ替えて、文を完成させましょう。

1. この道路標識は、ここでは駐車できないことを示しています。

[don't / this / you / road / here / shows / sign / park].

_____

2. そんなくだらないことを言うなんてあなたはなんて愚かなの！

[such / of / things / silly / you / to / how / say / foolish] !

_____

3. スコットランドにはなぜ来たのですか。

[brings / what / Scotland / to / you] ?

_____

GRAMMAR EXERCISE 2

日本語の意味になるように文を作ってみましょう。

1. 105 歳まで生きたとは彼女はなんて幸せなのだろう！

_____

2. 昨夜、あなたの家族に何が起きたのか聞かせてよ。

_____

DEFINITION FOR READING

1〜5の語句の定義として正しいものをa〜eから選んでみましょう。

1. administer (*l*.10) _____   a. to produce a particular substance in the body

2. secrete (*l*.14) _____   b. chemical compounds which affect some organs

3. hormone (*l*.12) _____   c. an interdependence of two or more things

4. correlation (*l*.23) _____   d. satisfaction, a condition of being contented

5. contentment (*l*.34) _____   e. to carry out, perform, or manage tasks

READING

DL 07   CD1-07 ~ CD1-11

次の文章を読み、あとに続く問題に答えましょう。

Dog Ownership and Mental Health Benefits

Dogs and humans have a special bond. In fact, there is evidence that the relationship between humans and dogs started over 15,000 years ago. We have evolved together and, as a result, are in tune with each other's emotions. It makes sense, then, that our moods can affect our dogs. A recent study

5 by scientists in Sweden, published in the journal *Nature*, provides strong evidence that this, indeed, might be the case.

The researchers investigated stress levels in humans and dogs. They studied a total of 58 dogs, both male and female, 33 Shetland Sheepdogs and 25 Border Collies. They also studied the dogs' owners. First, they assessed

10 the personalities of both the dogs and owners by administering personality tests. The owners took a personality test and filled one out for their dogs. The researchers also measured the amount of the hormone, cortisol, in the hair of the dogs and their owners over the course of one year.

Cortisol is secreted in the body when

15 there is physiological stress. Therefore, cortisol levels can be used as a way to measure stress in dogs and humans. If there are high amounts of cortisol present, a high level of stress is indicated. In this study, cortisol was measured

20 in the hair. Hair is a good way to measure

cortisol because it grows slowly at a rate of about one centimeter per month and absorbs cortisol from the blood. So, from hair, scientists can learn the amounts of cortisol in the blood over a long period of time and, by correlation, the amount of stress that was experienced.

The results of the study showed that there was a significant correlation 25 between cortisol in the owners and dogs over the year. That is, the changes in the cortisol levels of the dogs were very similar to those of their owners. While the personality of the dogs did not seem to affect the results, the personality of the owners did. Owners with a high amount of stress tended to have dogs with a high amount of stress, too. 30

We know the importance of taking care of the physical needs of our dogs, like giving them food and shelter, but we also need to think about their mental states. Dogs are able to experience both positive and negative emotions, such as contentment, happiness, fear and anxiety. We need to make sure our dogs have a balanced mental state. Interestingly, as this study 35 suggests, one of the best ways for us to help our dogs' mental health is by taking care of our own. By keeping ourselves mentally healthy, we keep our dogs healthy, too. A benefit of this, too, is that many things we can do to make ourselves happy are things we can do with our dogs. For example, taking a walk on the beach or in the mountains, playing in a park or just relaxing 40 together at home.

COMPREHENSION

次の文を読み、本文の内容と合っていればT、そうでない場合はFを選択しましょう。

1. Both the owners and dogs respectively answered their personality tests.

[T / F]

2. When you examine a dog's hair, you can guess its stress levels.

[T / F]

3. The personality of dogs and owners have nothing to do with the results.

[T / F]

4. If you do something good for you, you can do it for your dog too.

[T / F]

MAKE A SUMMARY

内容に合うように下線部に適切な語句や文を入れ、要約を完成させましょう。

Since humans and dogs have lived together, our moods have affected our dogs. Recent research investigated [1]_____ _____ to examine whether humans affect dogs. The amount of the hormone cortisol was measured in both to [2]_____. The result showed that [3]_____ between cortisol in both, especially for owners with [4]_____. We need to think about the mental health of our dogs as well as their physical needs, and we need to [5]_____ to keep our dogs healthy too.

HAVE YOUR SAY

以下は "Have you ever had any experience to share your mood with your pets?" という問いに対する、ある学生の回答です。ペアを組み、下線部を自分たちに置き換えて、配布された記入用紙に書いてみましょう（その後、クラスで発表してみましょう）。

> When I was a high school student, I had a cat. Do you know what it's really like owning cats? They are usually very shy, but my cat came to me every time I went to bed. She was good and cute. However, when I was angry or paid no attention to her, she never came to me. For example, once I was angry at chores and told her "Come here Milo!," she wouldn't move and hid her face instead. I didn't know how big her stress was at that time.

Unit

2 Virtual Relationship

ヴァーチャルな関係を長続きさせるには

 ISTENING

TARGET!

音の脱落・弱形を聞き取りましょう　　　🎧 DL 09　◎ CD1-13

1. 脱落＝同じ、または似た音が続くときに音が抜け落ちること

同じ音が続く	hot tea　take care　some more　orange juice　about time
似た音が続く	good time　with them　with that　next stop　hard time
破裂音＋破裂音	big doll　food processor　white jacket　sound change
破裂音＋鼻音	next month　right now
破裂音 + 摩擦音	hard feelings　at that　take those

2. 弱形＝英語を発音するリズムの中で語の音が弱くなること

機能語は弱く 発音される	Is he coming too?　It's not your fault.　What are you up to? I can't stand it any more.　You should have come earlier.

※「機能語」とは内容に関係のない語。「内容語」とは内容を伝える語で文の中で強く発音される

WARM UP　　　🎧 DL 10　◎ CD1-14

1〜5の文を聞き、音が脱落・弱形している箇所すべてに下線を引いてみましょう。

1. Did you ask her to come here?

2. I had a hard time finding a part-time job.

3. Would you like a cup of tea?

4. I am on my way to a job interview now.

5. You must get off at the next station.

TRY LISTENING　　　🎧 DL 11　◎ CD1-15

次の文を聞いて、（　　）に入る部分を補って文を完成させましょう。

What (　　　　) (　　　　　　) been doing lately? I am writing this email while

drinking a (　　　　　) (　　　　　　) (　　　　　　　　) at home. I've got an airline

ticket to London so I can see (　　　　　) (　　　　　) month. I (　　　　　　)

(　　　　　) reserved it much earlier. Where shall we go together? (　　　　　)

(　　　　　) a reply as soon as possible. (　　　　) (　　　　　)!

9

CONVERSATION

A. 次の会話を聞き、（　　）に適切な語を入れましょう。会話のあとに問題が流れるので、適切な答えを a、b から選びましょう。

Emiko is talking to Kim before class starts.

Emiko: Hi, Kim. What are you up to?

Kim: Just texting my boyfriend. [1]＿＿＿＿＿＿＿＿＿＿＿＿＿＿＿＿＿＿＿＿＿＿＿＿, so we are making plans.

Emiko: Oh, [2]＿＿＿＿＿＿＿＿＿＿＿＿＿＿＿＿＿＿＿＿? What are you guys going to do?

Kim: Yes. We are both going to order pizza and then eat together while video chatting. Then we are going to take a walk together after dinner.

Emiko: By video?! Sounds romantic! You've been dating for a while now, right?

Kim: For about six months. Actually, [3]＿＿＿＿＿＿＿＿＿＿＿＿＿＿＿＿＿＿＿ but he says he just wants us to be together online.

Emiko: Really? That's strange! I wonder why.

Kim: He says he's shy and [4]＿＿＿＿＿＿＿＿＿＿＿＿＿＿＿＿＿＿. The fact is we are both really enjoying our time together online so [5]＿＿＿＿＿＿＿＿＿＿＿＿＿＿＿＿＿＿. But I do want to meet him someday. How about you, Emiko, you're in a long-distance relationship, aren't you?

Emiko: Yes. My boyfriend goes to university in a different city. We haven't seen each other in ages. Maybe we should try an online date, too!

Q1.　**a.** She and her boyfriend will have pizza at the restaurant.
　　　b. She will chat with her boyfriend online while eating pizza.

Q2.　**a.** She isn't interested in meeting someone in person at all.
　　　b. She hasn't seen her boyfriend for a long time.

B. クラスメートとペアを組み、完成した会話を発話練習してみましょう。

C. ＿＿＿部を参考に、同じペアで次の①または②のシチュエーションで会話をしてみましょう。

① 彼らは夏休みにオーストラリアに行く予定なので、荷物を詰めているところだ。

② 彼はレポートをもうすぐ出す予定だが、まったくアイデアが浮かばず困っている (*be at a loss*)。

SHORT ANNOUNCEMENT

DL 13　CD1-17

A. 次の宣伝メッセージを聞き、下線部に適切な語句を入れましょう。

Introducing WhizU, an online meeting app. We make video conferencing and messaging across any device smooth and simple. With full HD video and audio, your meetings are sure to be clear. The app supports

1 _____, with full encryption

for all connections, so you can feel completely secure 2 _____

_____. The app also offers recording and auto-generated transcript options, so you don't need to take notes during meetings. All videos and transcripts can be uploaded to our cloud system and accessed for up to 20 years. We also offer virtual backgrounds so you can personalize our online meeting space and our sophisticated software automatically touches up your appearance to ensure you always look your best! Whether it is a one-to-one talk, an online class or office meeting,

3 _____, WhizU is here to help.

B. 次の文がメッセージの内容に合致している場合は T、そうでない場合は F を選択しましょう。

1. You can hold an online meeting with up to 2,000 participants by using WhizU.　　　　　　　　　　　　　　　　　　　　　　　　[T / F]

2. WhizU can help us to personalize an online meeting space.　[T / F]

3. You can enjoy any type of online communication with WhizU.　[T / F]

C. ペアを組み、　　部を参考に次のような内容で相手を説得してみましょう。必要に応じて自分たちで情報を付け加えて話しましょう。

> ・語彙力と少し大胆さがあれば、あなたの文章はきっとより正確になります。
> ・快晴でも雨でも曇り空でも、この防水仕様（water-proof）のランタンはあなたのお役に立ちます。

READING

動詞の種類と特殊な用法を学び、表現の幅を広げましょう

1. 自動詞と他動詞＝自動詞は目的語をとらない、他動詞は目的語をとる

他動詞と取違やすい自動詞　reply, apologize, look, listen など

自動詞と取違やすい他動詞　resemble, reach, approach, attend, consider, answer など

自動詞にも他動詞にも用いられる動詞　grow, sell, dream など

（自）Her latest novel is **selling** well.

（他）This store **sells** almost everything for gardening.

2. 使役動詞と知覚動詞

（使役）I couldn't **make** myself understood in English.

（知覚）I **felt** my heart beating fast in front of the large audience.

3. 提案や要求を表す動詞 ＋ that ＋ S ＋ 動詞の原形　※ should が省略されている

The instructor **insisted** that we [should] <u>be</u> cooperating with each other.

The doctor **suggested** that he [should] <u>do</u> moderate exercise every day.

GRAMMAR EXERCISE 1

日本語を参考に［　　］内の語句を並べ替えて、文を完成させましょう。

1. 顧客サービススタッフは発送の遅れについて私に謝罪した。

[delay / service / to / staff / customer / for / apologized / the / me / the] in shipment.

_____

2. 犠牲者の家族はその記事の削除を要求した。

[of / that / article / the / families / be / demanded / the victims / removed].

_____

3. だれもメアリーが教室から出ていったことに気づかなかった。

[of / noticed / out / nobody / classroom / going / Mary / the].

_____

GRAMMAR EXERCISE 2

日本語の意味になるように文を作ってみましょう。

1. 私の誕生日パーティーの前に部屋を掃除するのを手伝ってもらえますか。

_____

2. 私は家電量販店でコンピューターを修理してもらった。

_____

DEFINITION FOR READING

1〜5の語句の定義として正しいものをa〜eから選んでみましょう。

1. abundance (*l*.2) _____

2. exclusively (*l*.8) _____

3. intimacy (*l*.10) _____

4. mundane (*l*.17) _____

5. obstacle (*l*.36) _____

a. something that blocks your progress or achievement

b. ordinary and not interesting or exciting

c. a very large quantity of something

d. without others being included

e. a state of having a close personal relationship with someone

READING

🎧 DL 14   ◎ CD1-18 〜 ◎ CD1-22

次の文章を読み、あとに続く問題に答えましょう。

Maintaining an Online Relationship

With help of technology, the ways of developing and maintaining relationships are changing. There is an abundance of dating apps and websites to help people meet one another. Also, with multiple social media services and online tools, communication across long distances has never been easier. As a result, the number of online relationships is increasing. In   5
a recent survey, 20% of teenagers reported that they would be happy in an online-only relationship and, of those already in relationships, 10% reported that they communicate exclusively online. So, what can be done to help an online relationship grow? Three things that will help foster an online relationship are maintaining connection, building intimacy and creating a   10
future together.

First, it is important to maintain a connection with each other. Try and communicate with each other daily. You can set a time each day to talk on the phone or send text messages to each other. You can also use free apps like Facebook Messenger or LINE to avoid expensive phone bills. Also, try and   15
share as much about yourselves with each other as you can. Talk about your background, interests and dreams. Share the mundane things that happen each day, as well. Talk about your daily schedules, too. This will help you feel connected throughout the day.

Next, build intimacy. One way to do this is by having a video chat   20
at least once a week. Seeing each other's faces will help you feel closer to

each other. You can also do activities together while you are online. For example, you can eat dinner together or take a walk while having a video chat. Similarly, you can find fun things to do together like play online games or listen to music. Try and watch the same shows or read the same books and then talk about them. Another thing that will help build intimacy is if you send each other a personal item that will help you remember each other, like a T-shirt, stuffed toy, or some other cherished item.

Lastly, it is important to work on creating a future together. Talk with each other about what you want for the future. Setting goals and completing them will bring stability and confidence to your relationship. For example, you can make plans to have an online celebration and send each other gifts if your relationship lasts for a certain period of time. While some people in online relationships are happy to have the relationship entirely online, others hope to meet in person someday. For those who want to meet face to face, there might be obstacles, so you don't need to rush it. But working towards meeting up can give your relationship a sense of purpose.

Of course, maintaining an online relationship is sometimes hard. But with all the tools of technology available, it is not as difficult as it used to be. Maybe you are separated from your partner because you go to different universities. Maybe you have had to move to another city. Or maybe you just want to keep the communication online. Whatever the reason, if you work at it, and be patient and honest with each other, you can make the relationship succeed.

COMPREHENSION

次の文を読み、本文の内容と合っていれば T、そうでない場合は F を選択しましょう。

1. Twenty percent of teenagers reported that they communicate only online.

[T / F]

2. For maintaining connection, you need to communicate online at the same time every day.

[T / F]

3. Meeting in person is the most effective way to build intimacy.

[T / F]

4. Maintaining an online-only relationship is becoming easier than it used to be.

[T / F]

MAKE A SUMMARY

 DL 15   CD1-23

内容に合うように下線部に適切な語句や文を入れ、要約を完成させましょう。

    Thanks to developing social media services and online tools, online communication has become much easier than before. There are three steps for ¹_____. First, you need to maintain a connection with each other by sharing your ²_____, _____, _____ as well as everyday matters. Second, in order to ³_____, you should see each other and do something together by video chat. Third, working on ⁴_____ is quite beneficial. If you set the same goals and complete them, it ⁵_____ _____ to your relationship. By making use of all the technological tools available now, we are free to enjoy and maintain a fruitful online relationship.

HAVE YOUR SAY

以下は "Have you ever had any experience to communicate with someone only online?" という問いに対するある学生の回答です。ペアを組み、これを自分たちに置き換えて、下線部を書き換えてみましょう（その後、クラスで発表してみましょう）。

>   I have been <u>playing the game Go online with a girl</u> in <u>Singapore</u>. Her(His) name is <u>Sherry</u> and she(he) <u>has been playing Go for more than five years by social media</u>. <u>Playing Go with her</u> makes me <u>very happy but sometimes nervous</u> because <u>she is a famous Go instructor in her country</u>. I decided to <u>get better at playing Go to meet her standard</u>.

Changing Words over Time

時代とともに変わる言葉

 ISTENING

TARGET!

短縮・省略された音声に注意して聞き取りましょう　🎧 DL 16　💿 CD1-24

1. be 動詞・助動詞の短縮

He's (= He is, He has) / I'm (= I am) / You're (= You are) / I'd (= I would) / I've (= I have)

※'s にはほかに所有格もあるので文脈で見分ける必要があります

He's (he has) gone shopping.　　He's (he is) sleeping.

2. 否定形 not の短縮

isn't (= is not) / aren't (= are not) / don't (do not) / doesn't (does not)

3. 単語の一部を省略したもの（口語用法）

flu (= influenza) / ad (= advertisement) / sec (= second) / uni (= university)

4. 頭文字をとった省略（口語用法）

ASAP (= as soon as possible) / FYI (= for your information) / UK (= United Kingdom)

5. 音声に合わせた短縮表記（口語用法）

gonna (= going to) / wanna (= want to) / Gotcha! (= I got you.)

WARM UP　🎧 DL 17　💿 CD1-25

次の会話には短縮形が 4 箇所あります。それらをすべて抜き出し、その正式表記を右に書きましょう。

1. 短縮形（　　　）→ 正式（　　　　　　）　**2.** 短縮形（　　　）→ 正式（　　　　　　）

3. 短縮形（　　　）→ 正式（　　　　　　）　**4.** 短縮形（　　　）→ 正式（　　　　　　）

TRY LISTENING　🎧 DL 18　💿 CD1-26

次の文を聞いて、下線部に入る部分を補って文を完成させましょう。

I had a touch of the (　　　　　　　　) last night. Today I have a slight fever but I (　　　　) go to my (　　　　　　) to meet a friend I haven't seen in a long time. (　　　　　　　) studying for a (　　　　　　　　) in Health Science in Geneva while also working part-time at (　　　　　　). (　　　　　　) only stay in Japan until tomorrow so I (　　　　　) (　　　　　　) miss the chance to see her.

CONVERSATION
🎧 DL 19 💿 CD1-27

A. 次の会話を聞き、（　）に適切な語句や文を入れましょう。会話のあとに問題が流れるので、適切な答えをa、bから選びましょう。

Paul met his classmate James on campus.

Paul: Hey bro, ¹_____?

James: Great! I'm so excited. I just got tickets to the Sam Jones concert! Have you heard of them?

Paul: No, I haven't. ²_____ _____ that I've fallen behind with the latest music. What kind of music do they make?

James: Mostly pop. Maybe you've heard their song "We'll Last Forever". ³_____ online for the last few months.

Paul: Sorry, no. I just haven't been listening to much music lately. How many members are in the group?

James: Oh, ⁴_____, _____.

Paul: Really? But you kept saying "they" when you were talking about them.

James: Oh, yeah. Sam Jones prefers to be labeled as "they" rather than "he". It's because he considers himself to be nonbinary, ⁵_____ _____.

Paul: Oh, I guess I really am behind with things. That's interesting. The times are changing, aren't they?

Q1. a. It's a famous music band that consists of three members.
b. It's a name of a music unit but there's only one person.

Q2. a. Sam Jones doesn't want to be labeled by sex.
b. Sam Jones thinks themselves as more than a human being.

B. クラスメートとペアを組み、完成した会話を発話練習してみましょう。

C. ＿＿部を参考に、同じペアで次の①または②のシチュエーションで会話をしてみましょう。

① 以前にこの映画を見たことがあるかを聞く → 一度も見たことがない

② 今までにTOEICテストを受験したことがあるかを聞く → □回受験した（回数は自分で入れる）

17

SHORT ANNOUNCEMENT

A. 次の宣伝メッセージを聞き、下線部に適切な語句を入れましょう。

Tonight, on Entertainment Info, a message for everyone from megastar Sam Jones. Please do not address Jones with the pronouns "he" or "him". Tonight, the popular singer posted on social media a request to be referred to as "they" or "them". Jones wants fans to use these pronouns to avoid accidentally misgendering the artist. ¹_____ as genderqueer and nonbinary. Genderqueer people don't identify as conventionally male or female. Jones first announced they were nonbinary back in March of last year. In taking this step, Jones joins other pro singers such as Nora James and Steve Smith ²_____ _____ in an effort to create an accepting environment for all, ³_____. After the announcement, market sales of Jones' latest album, "Let's Go for a Drive", jumped up 15%. If you've not yet heard their music yet, it's definitely worth checking out!

B. 次の文がメッセージの内容に合致している場合は T、そうでない場合は F を選択しましょう。

1. Sam Jones asks fans not to address Jones with any pronouns.　　　[T / F]

2. Traditionally, genderqueer people don't identify themselves by their sex.
　　　[T / F]

3. The sales of Jones' latest album dropped sharply after the announcement.
　　　[T / F]

C. ペアを組み、　　　部を参考に次のような内容で、あるレストランの宣伝をしてみましょう。必要に応じて自分たちで情報を付け加えて話しましょう。

> ・予約なしで私たちのレストランには入店しないでください。
> ・当店の特製サンドイッチをまだ試していないのなら、絶対に試してみる価値があります。

READING

細かい時制表現を理解し、表現に磨きをかけましょう

1. 動詞の現在形を使う場合

（現在の状態）My parents **live** in Montreal.

（習慣的な動作）Susan always **refers** to Sam as 'they'.

（真理や社会概念）Cats **have** paws.

2. 過去形と現在完了＝ある過去の時点の動作は過去形で、現在まで続く動作は現在完了で表す

Janet **went** to Osaka yesterday. →今も大阪にいるかどうかは不明

Janet **has gone** to Osaka. →大阪へ行ったまま今も帰ってこない

3. 現在進行形と未来＝確定的な未来は現在進行形で表すことが多い

Sally **will move** to Seattle soon. / Sally **is moving** here in August.

GRAMMAR EXERCISE 1

日本語に合うように（　　）に適語を入れ、文を完成させましょう。

1. 私の母は寝る前にいつも K-POP を聞いている。

My mother always (　　　　　　　　) to K-POP before she (　　　　　　　).

2. 天気予報では明日は曇りだそうです。

The weather forecast (　　　　　　) it (　　　　　) (　　　　　)

cloudy tomorrow.

3.「キートンさんはどこだい？」「いますぐに来ますよ」

"Where (　　　　　　) Ms. Keaton?" "(　　　　　) (　　　　　)

right now."

GRAMMAR EXERCISE 2

日本語の意味になるように、与えられた語に続けるかたちで文を作ってみましょう。

1. 傘をなくしてしまったので、新しいのを買うつもりです。

Since _____, _____.

2. 私たちはその事件から歴史は繰り返すという事実を思い知らされた。

The incident _____.

DEFINITION FOR READING

1 〜 5 の語句の定義として正しいものを a 〜 e から選んでみましょう。

1. intimately (*l*.43)   _____   **a.** showing bravery and determination

2. valiant (*l*.4)   _____   **b.** dirty water or waste from homes and factories

3. sewage (*l*.21)   _____   **c.** very close, in a detailed way

4. nonconforming (*l*.35)   _____   **d.** future generations of humans

5. posterity (*l*.44)   _____   **e.** not in agreement with existing norms

READING

DL 21   CD1-29 ～ CD1-32

次の文章を読み、あとに続く問題に答えましょう。

Who is *They*?: The Evolution of English over Time

The English language is constantly changing. Like a river that never stops flowing, English words change and evolve. Words and language usage change to reflect changing cultural values and conditions. Merriam-Webster Inc., the well-established English dictionary company, makes a valiant effort
5
to catalogue these changes by updating their dictionary regularly. In 2019, for example, they added over 1,000 new words or definitions to their dictionary based on usage patterns. In some cases, the words were entirely new; in other cases, the meanings of words changed.

The new words added were quite varied. One new word added was
10
colorism, which is defined as "prejudice or discrimination especially within a racial or ethnic group favoring people with lighter skin over those with darker skin." Another word was *Bechdel test* which refers to a specific situation where the dialogue between two women does not concern a man. These words reflect a growing sensitivity for both gender and racial equality. Another word that
15
was added is quite disgusting: a *fatberg* is "a large mass of fat and solid waste that collects in a sewer system." The word is like the word iceberg and brings to mind something large that is floating in water.
20
The word *fatberg* originated in New York where there are a lot of sewage problems.

While there were many new words added to the English dictionary in 2019, a great many existing words had their usage changed. One notable example was the pronoun *they*. In fact, the word *they* was picked by Merriam-Webster as the word of the year in 2019. Along with its function as a plural third-person pronoun, the word *they* can now be "used to refer to a single person whose gender identity is nonbinary." According to Merriam-Webster, the number of times *they* was looked up in 2019 went up by a lot. This is partly due to celebrities like Sam Smith and Asia Kate Dillon choosing to refer to themselves with the pronoun *they* instead of *he* or *she*. According to the journalist, Molly Woodstock, "… they as a singular pronoun, as a pronoun for certain nonbinary folks is increasingly moving from only being talked about in queer and trans circles to the mainstream public consciousness." This official recognition of *they* came as a victory for many people who identify as nonbinary and gender nonconforming.

A similar change happened several hundred years ago with the word *you*. Originally, the second-person singular pronoun most used was *thou*. The word *you* was used only as a second-person plural pronoun. Gradually the situation changed, and people stopped using *thou* and started using *you* as a singular pronoun. At first it was difficult for people to adjust but eventually it became commonplace. The process of transformation that the English language is continually undergoing shows that language and culture are intimately connected. As culture changes, so does language. English is a living language that grows with the people using it. Our posterity will no doubt also look back and be fascinated by how words have changed.

COMPREHENSION

次の文を読み、本文の内容と合っていれば T、そうでない場合は F を選択しましょう。

1. Merriam-Webster Inc. has been regularly adding new words to their dictionary. [T / F]

2. The word *fatberg* refers to the excess fat in your body. [T / F]

3. The official recognition of *they* is largely due to celebrities who choose the word to refer to themselves. [T / F]

4. Long ago we used the word *thou* as a second-person plural pronoun. [T / F]

MAKE A SUMMARY

内容に合うように下線部に適切な語句や文を入れ、要約を完成させましょう。

　　The English language is changing over time like [1]_____

_____. Regularly, new words are added into dictionaries, such

as *colorism* and *fatberg*. Now, the pronoun *they* is used to refer to [2]_____

_____. The word [3]_____

_____ as the word of the year for 2019. In the same way,

the word *you* was once used as [4]_____,

but now the word can be used as both singular and plural second person

pronoun. As culture changes, so does language. English is a creature

[5]_____.

HAVE YOUR SAY

以下は "What do you think about the new meaning of *they*?" という問いに対
するある学生の回答です。ペアを組み、これを自分たちに置き換えて、下線部を書き
換えてみましょう（その後、クラスで発表してみましょう）。

　　Actually, I've never learned the new meaning of *they* until now.
But I think this meaning is <u>very fit for the times</u>. I have two nonbinary <u>friends in my uni</u> and <u>I am sometimes a bit confused as to
which pronoun to use when referring to either of them</u>.　From now
I can use the word *they/them*, so <u>I am really grateful for</u> this new
meaning.

Unit
4 Fika and Hygge

北欧式 心と体に良いくらし

LISTENING

TARGET!

様々な数字を使った表現を聞き取りましょう　🎧 DL 23　◎ CD1-34

年号・日付・時刻	2026 年（twenty twenty six / two thousand twenty six） 12 月 5 日（December fifth）　8 時 45 分（eight forty five / a quarter to nine）
序数	first, second, third, fourth, fifth ...　twelfth, thirteenth ... twenty-first
数式	6 x 8=48（Six times eight equals forty eight.） 15 ÷ 3=5（Fifteen divided by three equals five.）
分数	$\frac{1}{2}$（a half / one half）　$\frac{3}{7}$（three sevenths）　$4\frac{5}{8}$（four and five eighths）
金額	$11.50（eleven dollars and fifty cents / eleven fifty）
温度	28℃（twenty eight degrees Celsius） 114°F（one hundred fourteen degrees Fahrenheit）

数字に関する表現：a couple of days「2、3 日」 a decade「10 年」 a dozen「12」
　　　　　　　　two tablets a day after a meal「食後に一日 2 錠」

WARM UP　🎧 DL 24　◎ CD1-35

例のようにまず音声を聞き、そこで使われた数字表現を（　）に記入してみましょう。

（例）音声→ Today is August eighteenth.　答え→（　8 月 18 日　）

1. (　　　　　　　　)　2. (　　　　　　　　)
3. (　　　　　　　　)　4. (　　　　　　　　)
5. (　　　　　　　　)

TRY LISTENING　🎧 DL 25　◎ CD1-36

次の文を聞いて、下線部に入る部分を補って文を完成させましょう。

Yesterday I had a school reunion at a Chinese restaurant with _____ _____ alumni. It's been _____ since our graduation. We ate and talked from _____, and _____ stayed until _____. I have a headache today and need to take a tablet _____.

CONVERSATION

A. 次の会話を聞き、（　　）に適切な語句や文を入れましょう。会話のあとに問題が流れるので、適切な答えを a、b から選びましょう。

Erina is talking to Brandon while he's reading a book.

Erina: What are you reading, Brandon?

Brandon: It's a book about Hygge, a Northern European way of living that is quite in vogue now. The book gives advice about how to make your life more fulfilling.

Erina: Cool! I could use some advice about that, too. What does it say?

Brandon: Well, one thing it says is that we should spend less time on our smartphones. The average person spends
¹_____ on their phones.

Erina: Wow, I don't know if I could survive without my phone! The last time I checked my daily use it was about
²_____!

Brandon: Yeah, me too. My usage is often ³_____! Most of that time comes from watching YouTube and texting friends.

Erina: Sounds like we both could use a break from our phones!

Brandon: Yeah, another thing the book suggests is that it's important to
⁴_____. A good way to do this is to have coffee breaks with friends. The Swedes call theses breaks fika.

Erina: Hey, ⁵_____?

Brandon: Sure, and let's make sure not to use our phones while we're there!

Q1. **a.** It advises us to how we can live our lives with happiness and satisfaction.
b. It advises us never to use a smartphone while we are at home with family.

Q2. **a.** It means to have a break reading books with friends.
b. It means to relax having coffee breaks with friends.

B. クラスメートとペアを組み、完成した会話を発話練習してみましょう。

C. ＿＿＿部を参考に、同じペアで次の①または②のシチュエーションで会話をしてみましょう。

① 気分転換の重要性を説明するために、公園の散歩（take a walk）やジョギング（jog）を最善の方法として挙げる。

② 寝る前の運動（exercise）の重要性を説明するために、足裏マッサージ（foot massage）を最善の方法として挙げる。

SHORT ANNOUNCEMENT
DL 27 CD1-38

A. 次の宣伝メッセージを聞き、下線部に適切な語句を入れましょう。

We are happy to announce that a new coffee shop, Fika, will be opening at 12 locations around the city. At Fika, it's not just about enjoying incredible coffee, or sampling scrumptious sweets; it's about experiencing the homey atmosphere we create for you. Come with your friends and experience why the Nordic people love coffee breaks so much. Of course, with over ^{1}_____

_____, you will certainly find the combination that is perfect for you. Our founders, Lucas and Olivia, ^{2}_____

_____, have put their hearts and souls into creating a menu with the perfect combination of beverages and snacks to accompany whatever mood you might be in. Whether it is to relax with friends, do homework, or discuss business, we are waiting to serve you. Give our central branch a call at ^{3}_____ to find the closest shop near you.

B. 次の文がメッセージの内容に合致している場合は T、そうでない場合は F を選択しましょう。

1. At this shop, customers can experience a very modern Nordic atmosphere.

[T / F]

2. In this shop, there is a rich variety of coffee and desserts.

[T / F]

3. The founders of this shop have over forty years of business experience.

[T / F]

C. ペアを組み、＿＿部を参考に次のような内容でお店の宣伝をしてみましょう。必要に応じて自分たちで情報を付け加えて話しましょう。

> ・韓国スタイル（Korean style）の朝食を楽しむことができます。
> ・雨でも、晴天でも、曇り空でも来店をお待ちしています。

 **R**EADING

いろいろな助動詞を使いこなして表現をより豊かにしよう

基本の助動詞

can (could)	「〜できる」（可能） 「〜のはずだ」（推量・可能性）	must	「〜しなくてはならない」（強制・義務） 「〜にちがいない」（強い推量）
may (might)	「〜してもよい」（許可） 「〜かもしれない」（推量）	should	「〜すべきだ」（必要性・義務）

※未来を表す will も助動詞のひとつ。

助動詞と同じ働きをする語句

have to 「〜しなくてはならない」 / be able to 「〜できる」 / had better 「〜したほうが
よい、〜すべきだ」 / used to = would often 「〜したものだ」 / ought to 「〜すべきだ」

助動詞の慣用表現

cannot help ~ing 「〜せずにはいられない」 / may well 「〜するのはもっともだ」
cannot ~ too ... 「〜しすぎても ... すぎることはない」 / only have to ~ 「〜しさえすれ
ばよい」

GRAMMAR EXERCISE 1

日本文に合うように［　　］内の語句を並べ替え、<u>助動詞をひとつ加えて</u>文を完成さ
せましょう。

1. 昨夜の口論で彼はまだ怒っているかもしれない。

[night / still / the quarrel / he / angry / last / about / be].

_____

2. マリサがいつ職場復帰できるのか私たちにはわかりません。

[when / we / be / to / don't / Marisa / know / to / go / back / work / able].

_____

3. 娘が優勝したので、母親が彼女を誇りに思うのはもっともです。

[well / proud / be / daughter / of / Mother / her], as she got first prize.

_____

GRAMMAR EXERCISE 2

日本語の意味になるように文を作ってみましょう。

1. 私は以前アメリカのテレビドラマにはまっていたものだ。

_____

2. 今晩はあまり遅くまで起きていない方がよいでしょう。

DEFINITION FOR READING

1〜5の語句の定義として正しいものをa〜eから選んでみましょう。

1. hectic (*l*.7) _____   **a.** to remove unnecessary items

2. demeanor (*l*.15) _____   **b.** a promise to do something

3. declutter (*l*.21) _____   **c.** the way someone behaves, dresses and speaks

4. adorn (*l*.21) _____   **d.** very busy, full of activity

5. commitment (*l*.39) _____   **e.** to make more beautiful and attractive

READING

 DL 28   CD1-39 ～ CD1-43

次の文章を読み、あとに続く問題に答えましょう。

Hygge for Health

    With the stresses of modern life, people are looking for ways to improve their mental and emotional health. Hygge (pronounced hoo-ga) is a Danish term which, though hard to translate directly into English, combines the ideas of coziness, mindfulness, connection and hospitality. Hygge is a way of living that some people claim is the reason Nordic countries are considered some of   5 the happiest countries in the world. Hygge has become a popular alternative for people seeking to create less hectic lifestyles. So how do we live a hygge life?

    The main goal of hygge is to create a comfortable home environment where we can rest and recharge after a busy day. One of the first steps is   10 lighting. Try to use candles rather than electric lighting. While difficult in Japan, many Nordic people also use fireplaces to help warm up and light their homes. Along with lighting, keep some blankets on the sofas or chairs to create a cozy atmosphere. Try an evening by candlelight, wrapped in a blanket, and see if you notice a difference in your demeanor.   15

    Another important part of hygge is to create quiet time for yourself. An ideal way to do this is by reading books. Refrain from your computers and phones and spend some time reading a book that inspires you. Good books can open our minds and soothe our souls. Along with quiet time, to live a

20 hygge life, we should simplify our living space. Get rid of things you don't need. Decluttering your home will also declutter your mind. Similarly, adorn your home with things that are important to you, such as photos of family or friends or objects that bring to mind pleasant memories.

25 Maintaining good relationships is another aspect of hygge. Make time to spend with friends and family. The practice of *fika*, a Swedish term that means "coffee break," is another important part of the Nordic lifestyle. Setting aside time in the middle of a busy day to enjoy a cup of coffee with some friends or colleagues is a great way to boost your mood and energize you for the rest of the day. Similarly, try to have meals with people you enjoy being 30 around. Northern European people often have guests in their homes to enjoy meals together. Taking time to cook and share a meal together is another part of hygge that can enrich your life.

Finally, learn to appreciate what you have. Whether it is writing in a journal at the 35 end of the day or just taking time to remember the good things that happened to you, taking time to focus on being appreciative will greatly improve your mental and emotional well-being. Living a hygge life doesn't have to be a complete commitment or change of 40 lifestyle. Just taking time now and then to slow down and enjoy life with family and friends can be enough. Give hygge a try and learn a secret to health and happiness that the Nordic people have known for centuries.

COMPREHENSION

次の文を読み、本文の内容と合っていれば T、そうでない場合は F を選択しましょう。

1. Hygge is a way of life which combines coziness and mindfulness. [T / F]

2. To create a comfortable home environment, aroma is one important item. [T / F]

3. Reading even on a computer or smartphone is important to create a quiet time. [T / F]

4. To have a coffee break with friends and family in the day time is called *fika*. [T / F]

MAKE A SUMMARY

DL 29 CD1-44

内容に合うように下線部に適切な語句や文を入れ、要約を完成させましょう。

To improve our mental and emotional health, hygge life is becoming very popular among people. To create a ¹_____, lighting or your fireplace plays an important role. Moreover, having quiet time reading a book and ²_____ things such as photos or objects will work for hygge. To ³_____ _____ with people is also an important aspect. Taking time to ⁴_____ will improve our mental and emotional well-being. Hygge life ⁵_____ a complete commitment. Just enjoy life and we can learn a lot from the Nordic way of life.

HAVE YOUR SAY

以下は "What do you do when you have stress?" という問いに対するある学生の回答です。ペアを組み、これを自分たちに置き換えて、下線部を書き換えてみましょう（その後、クラスで発表してみましょう）。

Living in a modern society, we always face various kinds of stress. As a university student, I sometimes feel pressure when I have to do a presentation in front of the teacher and other students. Whenever I feel stress, I try to take a few deep breaths. It really works for me. Moreover, I think it is necessary to change my mood in order to get away from stress. I usually go running for an hour or so. It is very refreshing. Since we cannot live without stress, we need to learn how to deal with it.

Online Work Experience

オンラインで就活・インターン体験

 ISTENING

TARGET!

発音しにくい語やまぎらわしい語を聞き取りましょう 🎧 DL 30 ◎ CD1-45

日本人に発音しづらいものやカタカナ表記と異なるもの、表記があるのに発音しないものなどに注意しましょう。

a = /ei/	danger, angel, apron	ea = /e/	bread, meant, endeavor
ea = /iː/	beneath, disease, weave	ch = /k/	ache, epoch, chaos
ow = /au/	allow, cow, power, crown	e = /iː/	appreciate, compete, equal
o = /ou/	post, ghost, cold, local	o = /ʌ/	above, oven, among, love
oo = /ʌ/	blood, flood	oo = /u/	foot, book, hood, wool
gh = /f/	enough, laugh, draught	oa = /ou/	approach, boat, coal, float

[黙字] heir, honesty, honor, tomb, comb, calf, calm, folk, night, eight, taught

WARM UP

🎧 DL 31 ◎ CD1-46

次の音声を聞き、（　　）に適切な語を入れましょう。

1. I felt my (　　　　　　) begin to (　　　　　　).

2. He wasn't (　　　　　　) because he had his (　　　　　　) on.

3. The Sphinx is an (　　　　　　) guardian.

4. I (　　　　　　) your hospitality today.

　　—Don't mention it. It's my (　　　　　　).

5. My father reluctantly (　　　　　　) me to study abroad.

TRY LISTENING

🎧 DL 32 ◎ CD1-47

次の文を聞いて、（　　）に入る部分を補って文を完成させましょう。

Last (　　　　　　), heavy rains (　　　　　　) bad (　　　　　　) in my local town. (　　　　　　) I (　　　　　) (　　　　　　) to help my relatives and friends there, I could not go because of study commitments. However, many (　　　　　　) from other cities risked the (　　　　　) involved in removing (　　　　　　) to help. They also (　　　　　) many (　　　　　) blankets and (　　　　　) to the vicitms.

CONVERSATION

A. 次の会話を聞き、（　　）に適切な語句や文を入れましょう。会話のあとに問題
が流れるので、適切な答えを a、b から選びましょう。

Erina and Paul are chatting on the way home from class.

Erina: What are your plans for this summer, Paul?

Paul: I'll be heading home to stay with my parents.
And I'm also ¹_____

_____ .

Erina: From your hometown? Is there a company
there you'd like to work for?

Paul: Actually, I'm applying to companies in the
U.S. I'll be able to work on my English
² _____ .

Erina: How are you going to do that from your house? Online?

Paul: Exactly! Have you heard of Online Internships, Inc.?
³ _____ over the
internet from anywhere in the world. Right now, I'm taking a course
with them ⁴ _____ . Once I'm finished, they'll
send it out to companies of my choice and hopefully I'll get some offers!

Erina: That's fantastic! I should investigate that, too. ⁵ _____
_____ . I wonder if they have internships for that.

Paul: I'm sure they do. They have connections with all kind of companies all
over the world. And what's even better, most of the internships qualify
for university credit!

Q1. **a.** He is going to visit his hometown and stay there.
     b. He is planning to work in an office located in the U.S.

Q2. **a.** She wants to design software as an intern.
     b. She wants to learn about financial planning.

B. クラスメートとペアを組み、完成した会話を発話練習してみましょう。

C. ＿＿部を参考に、同じペアで次の①または②のシチュエーションで会話をしてみ
ましょう。

  ① 明日の試験に合格するかな→きっと合格するよ

  ② 彼らは無事に家に帰れたかな→どうだろう（さだかではない）

SHORT ANNOUNCEMENT

A. 次の宣伝メッセージを聞き、下線部に適切な語句を入れましょう。

Are you seeking an internship with a leading company but are unable to travel because of work or family obligations? At Online Internships, Inc., we are ready to help make your dream come true. We provide internship programs that [1]_____, without ever having to leave your home. Let us connect you with companies across the country or globe, [2]_____ _____, such as social media support, website design, market reporting, financial planning and much more. Through our programs, you'll forge global connections and build a professional network that is crucial to future success. You'll also gain valuable remote work skills, such as written communication and team problem solving, as well as developing proficiency in software and computing platforms connected to your chosen career. To help get you started, we also provide [3]_____.

Contact us today!

B. 次の文がメッセージの内容に合致している場合は T、そうでない場合は F を選択しましょう。

1. The company offers you a domestic internship program. [T / F]

2. This program has connections with various projects such as website design and marketing and so on. [T / F]

3. At first, the program offers how to write an interview report. [T / F]

C. ペアを組み、□□部を参考に次のようなプログラムの告知をしてみましょう。必要に応じて自分たちで情報を付け加えて話しましょう。

> ・海外の大学で様々な分野について学べる留学プログラム (overseas studying program) を提供しています。
> ・この留学プログラムを通して、様々な異文化を体験し、そして英語力を向上させることができるでしょう。

EADING

TARGET!

特殊な名詞とその用法を覚えましょう

1. 特殊な名詞

集合名詞	audience, committee, staff	抽象名詞	music, information, success
物質名詞	water, gas, wood, butter	固有名詞	Jack, Africa, Google, Monday

不可算名詞の例外→ waters（池や海）/ woods（森）/ advices（通達）

2. 注意すべき代名詞の用法

非人称の **it** = ①天候、時間、距離、状況 ②形式主語 ③形式目的語など
It will be sunny this afternoon. / We took **it** for granted that he would not agree.

不定代名詞 = one, another, some, any, both, other, either, neither
He bought **a** new bicycle. — I have **one** too. / **Both** apps are great, but I don't have **either**.

3. 冠詞 =不特定の単数可算名詞につく不定冠詞（a, an）、特定のものを表す定冠詞（the）
My father has **a Honda**. →「ホンダの車」/ Jim and I had **a good many** beers yesterday.
→「かなり多くの」

He hopes to help **the poor**. →「貧しい人々」/ Someone slapped me on **the back**.
→ the ＋（体の部分）

GRAMMAR EXERCISE 1
（　　）に適語を入れて、文を完成させましょう。

1. She prides (　　　　　　) on raising (　　　　　　) five children.
2. (　　　　　　) English are often said to be (　　　　　　) trustworthy people.
3. I felt someone tap (　　　　) on (　　　　) shoulder but no
 (　　　　)(　　　　) there.

GRAMMAR EXERCISE 2
日本語の意味になるように文を作ってみましょう。

1. 私の友人はこの近くには一人も住んでいない。
 [of / here / friends / live / none / my / near].

2. 研究者たちは 2 年前に発見された絵がピカソの作品であると確認した。
 Researchers [a / identified / years / painting / have / two / ago / as / found / the / Picasso].

DEFINITION FOR READING

1〜5の語句の定義として正しいものをa〜eから選んでみましょう。

1. pandemic (*l.*1)　　_____　　**a.** a period when a person is kept apart from others

2. peer (*l.*4)　　_____　　**b.** being attractive, useful; necessary course of action

3. quarantine (*l.*12)　　_____　　**c.** a person of the same age, status, or ability

4. desirable (*l.*31)　　_____　　**d.** to make an action or process possible or easier

5. facilitate (*l.*28)　　_____　　**e.** a disease that affects people over a very large area

READING

DL 35　CD1-50 ～ CD1-55

次の文章を読み、あとに続く問題に答えましょう。

Virtual Career Development

Society is evolving. The pressures of the recent COVID-19 pandemic have forced people to change their lifestyles. The need to work and attend school from home has pushed people to develop new skills and ways of interacting with their colleagues and peers. As a result, some universities
5　have adapted and developed new ways for students to go through the job-seeking process. Now it is possible for students to attend job fairs, internships and even eventually work, virtually, from the comfort and security of their homes.

Students looking for full-time jobs or internships now have new
10　opportunities through virtual job fairs. As an example, CareerEco job fair, which is normally open to 28 schools in the Southeastern United States, held its first online event in spring 2020. Because of COVID-19 quarantines, students were unable to physically attend the job fair, so it went virtual. By simply uploading their resumes, students had the opportunity for over 120
15　different employers to consider them for positions.　Similarly, in the same year, the Hiatt Career Center of Brandeis University moved all its services online. Along with arranging for students to virtually engage with employers, the center began offering services such as online interview coaching and resume building.

20　Beyond finding an internship online, there are a growing number of opportunities to do internships online as well. Latham & Watkins, an international law firm, has developed what they call Virtual Experience Programs (VEPs) which give participants online training as well as the chance to undertake legal work and find out what life is like at the company. There are currently two VEPs. The Acquisitions VEP takes participants through high-stakes transaction processes and the White-Collar Defense and Investigations VEP lets interns work through actual criminal investigations. 25

Companies are now being developed that focus solely on facilitating online internships, for example, Virtual Internship Partners, the UK's first virtual internship company. According to one of its cofounders, "We recognized that there was a whole desirable skill set that candidates can learn through a remote or virtual internship, and that this also reduces traditional barriers to internships, such as logistics, cost, family or study commitments, for a number of candidates." 30

Being able to overcome these traditional barriers certainly helped Luke McClendon, who recently completed a virtual internship through World Campus at Penn State. Along with pursuing his degree in health administration online, he was working 30 to 40 hours a week and raising a family. He was able to do an internship with the Alzheimer's Association and work remotely developing social media campaigns and working on volunteer program enrollment. Without the option to do the internship remotely, he might not have been able to arrange the time to do it at all. 35

40

These internships also pave the way to careers that involve remote work. With the advance of teleconferencing and telework technology, it's not uncommon for business to allow their employees to work from home several days a week. The social distancing made necessary by the COVID-19 pandemic may have expedited the process of moving to virtual workplaces, but society was already heading there. It remains to be seen how far this trend will continue. 45

COMPREHENSION

次の文を読み、本文の内容と合っていればT、そうでない場合はFを選択しましょう。

1. Nowadays most students seeking jobs should attend job fairs physically.

[T / F]

2. Virtual Experience Programs offer not legal work, but processing transaction and criminal investigations. [T / F]

3. Virtual internship candidates are free from the traditional barriers of typical internships. [T / F]

4. Luke McClendon obtained his degree online while working long hours to support his family. [T / F]

MAKE A SUMMARY

🎧 DL 36 💿 CD1-56

内容に合うように下線部に適切な語句や文を入れ、要約を完成させましょう。

Because of ^{1} _____, the way for students
^{2} _____ is changing.
Many companies come to offer opportunities for students to join online job fairs or to receive effective services such as ^{3} _____
_____. Furthermore, some companies provide services to help students to join online internship programs. As students can do an internship from their home, they can ^{4} _____
_____, such as logistics, cost, family obligations or study pressure. With ^{5} _____
_____, employees no longer need to come to the office every day. Not only students but also society itself is getting used to this new way of life and work.

HAVE YOUR SAY

以下は "Have you ever thought of learning something online?" という問いに対するある学生の回答です。ペアを組み、これを自分たちに置き換えて、下線部を書き換えてみましょう(その後、クラスで発表してみましょう)。

Actually I started to join a language-learning program online last month. It offers both one-to-one and group online conversation lessons and written tasks. Before I decided to join this program, I checked more than ten learning programs. Among them, I finally decided on one program because the teaching staff seem so efficient. They replied to my email soon after I asked questions. Now I have gotten accustomed to submitting online tasks and I really enjoy online conversation classes.

Unit 6

Fashion and Climate Change

ファッションと気候変動の関係とは？

Made with 100% Recycled Fabric

LISTENING

TARGET!

挨拶表現のバリエーションを学びましょう　🎧 DL 37　◎ CD1-57

出会いの挨拶

〈カジュアルな挨拶〉
Hi! / Hi, there! / Hello! （こんにちは） / What's new? / What's up? （調子はどう）
How are you (doing)? / How's it going? （元気ですか）

〈フォーマルな挨拶〉
Nice to meet you. / It's a pleasure to meet you. / Good to see you. （お会いできて嬉しいです）

〈久しぶりに会った場合〉
How have you been? （元気でしたか）　Long time no see. / It's been a while. （お久しぶりです）

別れの挨拶

〈カジュアルな挨拶〉
Bye. / See you. / See you later. （またね）　Take care. （体に気をつけて）

〈フォーマルな挨拶〉(It was) Nice meeting you. （お会いできてよかったです）

〈別れを切り出す〉I should get going. / Sorry, I got to run. （もう行かなくちゃ）

WARM UP
🎧 DL 38　◎ CD1-58

1～4の挨拶に対する返答として適切なものを、読まれる音声a～dから選びましょう。

1. Hi, there! How are you?　(　　　)　　**2.** Long time no see.　(　　　)

3. How have you been doing?　(　　　)　　**4.** Sorry, I got to run.　(　　　)

TRY LISTENING
🎧 DL 39　◎ CD1-59

男女の会話を聞いて、下線部に入る部分を補って文を完成させましょう。

A: Hey, aren't you Beth Martin from Jenison High School?

B: Oh, are you Roger Watkins? _____!

A: Indeed, _____. It's so _____ again.

B: Yeah, we should get together some time.

A: Let's do it. Here's my email address.

B: Thanks. Oh, _____. Bye!

CONVERSATION

A. 次の会話を聞き、（　　）に適切な語を入れましょう。会話のあとに問題が流れるので、適切な答えを a、b から選びましょう。

Julia is interviewing Craig for a podcast.

Julia: (host) Welcome to the Sustainably Stylish, a weekly podcast on sustainable fashion. I'm your host, Julia Marten, and today we have a very special guest, Craig Williams from Naturewear, a cutting-edge company that is developing new, environmentally friendly clothes. Welcome, Craig.

Craig: (guest) Thank you very much, Julia. [1]_____.

Julia: So first, Craig, could you tell us about this new material you and your team have developed?

Craig: Well, it's really quite exciting. We've taken palm leaves and, through a natural chemical process, developed a material that looks and feels like leather. We call it Palmex.

Julia: Fascinating! And [2]_____?

Craig: It functions just like real leather. We can use it in shoes, jackets, belts, even furniture! Furthermore, it's quite economical.

Julia: Amazing! And how about the environmental impact of this new material?

Craig: That's the best part! Manufacturing Palmex emits far less carbon dioxide than real leather, [3]_____, actually.

Julia: Wonderful! Well, [4]_____ today, Craig. [5]_____. And for our listeners, we'll be back after the break with more exciting fashion news.

Q1. **a.** It is made from leather, which does not emit carbon dioxide.
b. It is made from palm leaves through a natural chemical process.

Q2. **a.** The material to make it is very cheap and environmentally friendly.
b. It only emits almost the same amount of carbon dioxide as the real leather.

B. クラスメートとペアを組み、完成した会話を発話練習してみましょう。

C. ＿＿＿部を参考に、同じペアで次の①または②のシチュエーションで会話をしてみましょう。

① 「あなたとあなたの家族が目撃した事件（incident）について教えてください」

② 「あなたが最近はまっている（be into）ビデオゲームについて教えてください」

SHORT ANNOUNCEMENT

🎧 DL 41 ⊙ CD1-61

A. 次の宣伝メッセージを聞き、下線部に適切な語句を入れましょう。

Do you care about the effects your fashion choices have on the environment? Do you want to look your best? Well, so do we! Here at Naturewear, we strive to create clothing that makes you feel great, both in the way you look and the way you feel. Our products all have very low carbon footprints, so you can [1]_____

_____. And with our complete line of men's and women's clothing, you are sure to find the perfect ensemble to express your unique taste and style. We've also just introduced a new line of vegan leather clothing, featuring our new material, Palmex. Try out our new jackets, belts and shoes for the look and feel of leather made [2]_____

_____. Are you ready to take the next step towards helping the climate and looking great? Please visit our website at www.naturewear. com to find a store near you! [3]_____!

B. 次の文がメッセージの内容に合致している場合は T、そうでない場合は F を選択しましょう。

1. The products at Naturewear have no carbon footprints so they are environmentally friendly.   [T / F]

2. It is possible to coordinate both men's and women's line of clothes.   [T / F]

3. Palmex is a new material that feels like a real leather and can be used even for shoes.   [T / F]

C. ペアを組み、____部を参考に次のような内容で、ある自然食レストランの宣伝をしてみましょう。必要に応じて自分たちで情報を付け加えて話しましょう。

- 私たちはお客様に素晴らしい食体験と自然への貢献を感じられるようなメニューを作るべく努力しています。
- 動物を犠牲（scrifice）にすることなく、肉の見た目と食感を体験したいのでしたら、私たちの新しいヴィーガンレストランをお試しください。

READING

前置詞句でより細かいニュアンスを説明しましょう

前置詞句＝前置詞が他の語句と結合し特定の意味になるもの

〈**at**〉*be* good at ~「～が上手」 *be* poor at ~「～が下手」

〈**of**〉*be* made of ~「～でできている（材質）」 ※原材料の場合は *be* made from
in front of ~「～の前に」 because of ~「～のせいで」 instead of ~「～の代わりに」
be tired of ~「～にうんざりする」 *be* afraid of ~「～が怖い」

〈**in**〉*be* interested in~「～に興味がある」 in order to ~「～するために」

〈**to**〉thanks to ~「～のおかげで」 according to ~「～によると」

〈その他〉
judge from ~「～から判断する」 *be* familiar with ~「～をよく知っている」
worry about ~「～を心配する」 *be* famous for ~「～で有名である」など

GRAMMAR EXERCISE 1

前置詞をひとつ追加して [   ] 内の語句を並べ替え、文を完成させましょう。

1. They [game / the / the / result / soccer / were / so / of / upset].

_____

2. My mother [here / familiar / is / very / the / around / restaurants].

_____

3. I am [TV program / the / same / every day / watching / tired].

_____

GRAMMAR EXERCISE 2

日本語の意味になるように文を作ってみましょう。

1. あなたは何を恐れているのですか。

_____

2. 現在の状況から判断すると、私たちは試合に負けるでしょう。

_____

3. この紙は石だけでできているので、経済的で環境にもよいです。

_____

DEFINITION FOR READING

1〜5の語句の定義として正しいものをa〜eから選んでみましょう。

1. strive (*l*.4) ＿＿＿

2. predicament (*l*.9) ＿＿＿

3. buzzword (*l*.18) ＿＿＿

4. algae (*l*.26) ＿＿＿

5. photosynthesis (*l*.30) ＿＿＿

a. a phrase that has become fashionable

b. a difficult and unpleasant situation

c. very simple plant growing in or near water

d. the production by a green plant caused by the action of sunlight

e. to make a great effort to achieve something

READING

DL 42   ◎ CD1-62 ～ ◎ CD1-66

次の文章を読み、あとに続く問題に答えましょう。

Climate Positivity in Fashion

The fashion industry is being forced to evaluate its role in climate change. With evidence pointing towards an impending environmental crisis if carbon dioxide (CO_2) emissions are not curbed, clothing companies are striving to make their products more sustainable. Yet, even so, the amount of waste that comes from global textile production is staggering, with some studies estimating that the industry produces over 1.2 billion tons of carbon dioxide a year. That's more than the annual airline and maritime shipping emissions combined.

Considering this predicament, a new term has been proposed to replace the word sustainability: "climate positivity". With sustainability, the aim is to lower the amount of carbon emissions in the manufacturing process whereas, with climate positivity, the aim is to go beyond reducing the carbon footprint to actually create a benefit to the environment by eliminating carbon dioxide from the atmosphere. The term "climate positivity" was first introduced by the non-profit organization Slow Factory Foundation because of a perceived lack of clarity coming from many fashion companies about how sustainable their products are. According to the director of Slow Factory Foundation, "Sustainable fashion is becoming a buzzword but it doesn't mean anything. Brands are claiming sustainability left and right. And unfortunately, it's getting trapped at the surface in the marketing department, it's not trickling down deep, deeper into the roots of the problem."

5

10

15

20

So, what kinds of processes could be considered climate positive? In fact, there are some very interesting developments being made in textile manufacturing that could revolutionize the way clothing is designed. For example, Charlotte McCurdy, a fashion designer from New York, recently designed a raincoat made from algae. Algae can draw carbon out of the atmosphere, so this raincoat actually cleans the environment as it is worn. Algae is being used by other designers, as well. For instance, Post Carbon Lab, a start-up based in London has developed a coating of algae that can be applied to fabric. Through photosynthesis, this coating absorbs carbon dioxide from the atmosphere and emits oxygen. According to the company, one large T-shirt with this coating generates as much oxygen as a six-year old oak tree. Eventually, it is speculated that this coating could be used on shoes, jackets, backpacks, curtains and other products. Of course, algae-based clothing needs special care. The clothing is damaged by washing machines, so it needs to be handwashed. Also, algae need light and carbon dioxide to survive so the clothing should be put in a well-ventilated area.

Another advancement that could be considered climate positive is the development of leather substitutes. Examples are Pinatex, made from pineapple leaves, Mycotex, made from mushrooms, and Desserto, made from cactus. The leather industry puts a huge strain on the environment so using plant products, instead, helps create a cleaner atmosphere.

With such innovations, the fashion industry has the potential to go from being part of the environmental problem to being part of the solution. While the clock is ticking in regard to how much time we have to avert climate change, solutions are being developed that give us reasons to be hopeful.

COMPREHENSION

次の文を読み、本文の内容と合っていれば T、そうでない場合は F を選択しましょう。

1. Carbon dioxide from textile production industry is almost equal to that of annual airline and maritime shipping emissions combined.　　　[T / F]

2. The term "climate positivity" was first introduced by the fashion market.

[T / F]

3. Algae clothing has to be handwashed and needs to be stored in a well-ventilated place. [T / F]

4. As a substitution for leather, the leather industry is making an effort by using plants. [T / F]

MAKE A SUMMARY

 DL 43 CD1-67

内容に合うように下線部に適切な語句や文を入れ、要約を完成させましょう。

　　Clothing companies are now striving to make their products more sustainable and trying to reduce the amount of ¹＿＿＿＿＿＿＿＿＿＿＿ ＿＿＿＿＿＿＿＿ in the manufacturing process. The term "climate positivity" has been introduced by Slow Factory Foundation to clarify ²＿＿＿＿＿＿＿ ＿＿＿＿＿＿＿＿＿＿＿＿＿＿＿＿. There are some interesting developments, for example, Charlotte McCurdy designed a raincoat made from algae. Since algae ³＿＿＿＿＿＿＿＿＿＿＿＿＿＿＿＿＿＿, the raincoat actually cleans the environment as it is worn. Another advancement is ⁴＿＿＿＿＿＿＿＿ ＿＿＿＿＿＿＿＿＿＿＿＿＿. The leather industry puts a huge strain on the environment. So using plant products, instead, helps ⁵＿＿＿＿＿＿＿＿, ＿＿＿＿＿＿＿＿＿＿＿＿＿. It shows that the fashion industry still has the potential to go further.

HAVE YOUR SAY

以下は "As a consumer in fashion industry, what can we do to protect the environment?" という問いに対する、ある学生の回答です。ペアを組み、下線部を自分たちに置き換えて、配布された記入用紙に書いてみましょう（その後、クラスで発表してみましょう）。

> Lately, the fashion industry has been trying to do a lot of things to protect the environment. This is something we, as consumers, need to take seriously. For example, I don't <u>buy products that use a certain kind of fur</u> or <u>choose products with fake fur</u>. Moreover, we could <u>buy</u> clothing <u>which is recycled</u>, since the resources on earth are limited. Also, we shouldn't buy clothes that <u>we would throw away in a short time</u>. I think it's important to choose clothing that <u>you can wear for a long time</u>. We need to think whether we really need it before we buy.

Unit 7 Can We Travel to Space?

宇宙旅行の実現はいつ？

LISTENING

TARGET!

依頼・勧誘表現のバリエーションを学びましょう　🎧 DL 44　💿 CD1-68

1. カジュアルな表現

Will you check the schedule of tomorrow's meeting? – Of course. / Sure.

Let's (Shall we) go for dinner tomorrow. (?) / **How about** going for a walk?

Why don't we take a break? / **Why not** ask him if he's got a girlfriend?

2. 丁寧な表現

Could you finish recording the video by tomorrow? – OK, I will do my best.

Would you mind turning on the air conditioning? – No problem. / No, not at all.

Would you do me a **favor**? / May I ask you a **favor**? / I have a **favor** to ask you.

（より控えめな依頼）

I was wondering if you could have dinner with us.

I would be grateful if you could help me with my activities.

WARM UP　🎧 DL 45　💿 CD1-69

1 ～ 4 の音声を聞き、その返答として適切なものを A、B から選びましょう。

1. A. I can tell you why.　**B.** No, not at all.

2. A. I'm afraid I'll be off campus on that day.　**B.** Yes, I enjoyed the party too.

3. A. Not so much. Why?　**B.** Sure, what?

4. A. Of course, please try one.　**B.** I'd love to, but I don't have time.

TRY LISTENING　🎧 DL 46　💿 CD1-70

1 ～ 5 の問いかけに対する返答として適切なものを、読まれる音声 a ～ e から選びましょう。

1. We have a farewell party next Sunday. Can you join us?　（　　）

2. Would you mind my borrowing your textbook?　（　　）

3. Excuse me, show me your ID please.　（　　）

4. I would be grateful if you could respond to my email soon.　（　　）

5. Please let me know if you have any suggestions.　（　　）

CONVERSATION

DL 47 · CD1-71

A. 次の会話を聞き、（　　）に適切な語を入れましょう。会話のあとに問題が流れるので、適切な答えを a ～ c から選びましょう。

Paul and Erina are chatting before class starts.

Paul: Did you hear the news?

Erina: What news?

Paul: Space Tours Inc., the pioneer in private space travel, is having a raffle for two seats on their first private flight into space!

Erina: Wow, that's amazing! Normally tickets cost a fortune, don't they?

Paul: They sure do. The event was announced yesterday at [1]＿＿＿＿＿＿＿＿＿＿＿＿＿＿＿＿＿＿＿＿＿＿＿＿＿. [2]＿＿＿＿＿＿＿＿＿＿＿＿＿＿＿＿＿＿＿＿＿＿＿? I've already bought five!

Erina: Five? How much are they? How do you buy them? I'd definitely like to get some [3]＿＿＿＿＿＿＿＿＿＿＿＿＿＿＿＿＿.

Paul: They're only $20.00 each, which is pretty cheap considering what you can win. You can easily get them online.

Erina: Alright! I'll get five, too, I think. I'd get more but that's all I can afford. If you win, you'll invite me, too, right?

Paul: Of course! And if you win, [4]＿＿＿＿＿＿＿＿＿＿＿＿＿＿＿＿＿＿＿＿?

Erina: Absolutely! So, [5]＿＿＿＿＿＿＿＿＿＿＿＿＿＿＿＿＿＿＿!

Paul: Can you imagine how amazing it would be to see the Earth from space? We would be a part of history!

Erina: I'd better get online and get those tickets. I'm so excited!

Q1   **a.** twice a year   **b.** once a month   **c.** five times

Q2   **a.** 20 dollars   **b.** 200 dollars   **c.** 100 dollars

B. クラスメートとペアを組み、完成した会話を発話練習してみましょう。

C. ＿＿部を参考に、同じペアで次の①または②のシチュエーションで会話をしてみましょう。

① もしあなたが負けたら、私にピザをおごってくれる？→いいよ

② もし明日が晴れなら、私たちをピクニックへ連れていってくれる？→いいよ。それでもし雨なら、私の宿題のお手伝いをお願いしてもいい？

SHORT ANNOUNCEMENT

 DL 48 CD1-72

A. 次のスピーチを聞き、下線部に適切な語句を入れましょう。

Hello everyone and welcome. We are delighted that you could join us today as we have a very special announcement. As you know, we at Space Tours Inc. have been striving to develop some of the first commercial flights to space and we are thrilled to tell you today, that ¹_____ _____ for our first commercial flight out past the stratosphere! We will be taking six citizens on a historic private flight to our space station orbiting Earth. ²_____ _____ but we are excited to tell you that we will be opening up the remaining two seats for raffle! Starting today, you can buy tickets from our website and, at the end of the month, we will choose two lucky winners to make the journey to space! ³_____ _____ devoted to underprivileged children. Why don't you get some tickets, today?

B. 次の文がメッセージの内容に合致している場合は T、そうでない場合は F を選択しましょう。

1. The date of the flight was set for July 2020 but it will be changed. [T / F]

2. More than half of the flight seats are already taken. [T / F]

3. You can get your money back if you do not win the raffle. [T / F]

C. ペアを組み、 ___ 部を参考に次のような内容で、あるコーヒー専門店の宣伝をしてみましょう。必要に応じて自分たちで情報を付け加えて話しましょう。

> ・明日から、どのコンビニでも当社の特製オーガニックコーヒー（special organic coffee）を購入することができます。そして年末には、オーガニックコーヒー専門店をオープンする予定です！
> ・この 12 月に来店して、当社のコーヒーを試してみませんか。

READING

形容詞・副詞の機能と種類を学んで使いこなしましょう

形容詞＝名詞を修飾

1. 限定用法＝名詞の前に置く。限定用法のみ　only, very, western, main, total など
This is the **only** symptom of the disease. / She is an **enthusiastic** student.

2. 叙述用法＝補語（C）になる。叙述用法のみ　awake, afloat, alive, alone, worth など
限定用法と叙述用法で意味が変わるもの
〈late〉I was **late** for her party.「遅れた」/ My **late** sister was a nurse.「故〜、今は亡き」

3. 分詞形容詞＝分詞が独立して形容詞となったもの。
The game was **exciting**. / That was a very **surprising** outcome.

副詞＝動詞、形容詞・副詞、文を修飾

1. 動詞を修飾するもの　always, carefully, slowly, completely
否定の意味を含むもの　seldom, never, hardly, scarcely, rarely など

2. 形容詞・副詞を修飾するもの very, so, almost など

3. 文を修飾するもの（話し手の主観を表す）clearly, probably, fortunately など
Luckily, I won a ticket to the moon. / **Fortunately,** she was not in her room then.

GRAMMAR EXERCISE 1

[　　] 内の語句を並べ替え、文を完成させましょう。

1. Since the accident, [in / is / again / afraid / Kenji / water / to / go / too / the].

_____

2. [so / was / I / when / filmmaker / I / late / delighted / the / interviewed]
years ago.

_____

3. [museum / the / all / the / were / almost / in / created / works] in the
18th century.

_____

GRAMMAR EXERCISE 2

日本語の意味になるように文を作ってみましょう。

1. 結局、私たちは京都へ新幹線で行くことにしました。

_____

2. 幸運なことに、その病気で死に至ることはめったにない。

_____

DEFINITION FOR READING

1〜5の語句の定義として正しいものをa〜eから選んでみましょう。

1. arguably (*l*.9)   _____   **a.** being over the speed of sound

2. affordable (*l*.3)   _____   **b.** able to be bought, not so expensive

3. supersonic (*l*.38)   _____   **c.** in a severe or serious way

4. pave the way (*l*.33)   _____   **d.** in a way that can be appeared to be true

5. drastically (*l*.40)   _____   **e.** to make progress

READING

DL 49   CD1-73 ~ CD1-77

次の文章を読み、あとに続く問題に答えましょう。

Space Tourism is No Longer Just a Dream

Planning a vacation can be an exciting process. Modern airline technology makes it possible to go nearly anywhere on the planet in an affordable and time-efficient manner. However, in the upcoming years, options for travel are going to expand even more. Once only the speculation of science-
5 fiction writers, space tourism is now a reality. Soon, it will be possible to plan a vacation into outer space, or even another planet! Companies are already planning first trips for space tourists.

One such company, SpaceX, founded by billionaire entrepreneur Elon Musk, is arguably
10 one of the best-known private space companies. In March 2020, the company announced that it will send three tourists to the International Space Station (ISS) for ten days in late 2021. The trip won't be cheap, though, with tickets
15 costing $55 million. This mission will be the first completely private trip to the ISS and became possible after NASA announced that it would start opening the ISS to more commercial activities such as space tourism. SpaceX has even more ambitious goals, however.

    Currently, the company plans to send Yusaku Maezawa, the founder of
20 Zozotown, Japan's largest online fashion mall, to the moon in 2023. Maezawa will be the first visitor to the moon since the U.S. Apollo mission in 1972. And

Maezawa won't be travelling alone; he plans to invite up to eight top artists from around the world to go with him with all expenses paid. The artists will be asked to create artworks reflecting their experiences and Maezawa believes the artworks will be an inspiration for the entire human race. But even taking Maezawa to the moon isn't the end of SpaceX's aspirations. They have projected that they will be able to take people to Mars as early as 2024! 25

Another company that is making a name for themselves in space tourism is Virgin Galactic. The organization plans to launch the first private space tourism flight by the end of 2020. After a disastrous accident in 2014 where a ship crashed and a pilot was killed, in 2018, the company rebounded and successfully launched a vehicle that carried Virgin Galactic's first passenger into space. This success paved the way for the commercial flights currently in development. Already, nearly 700 customers have paid the $200,000 cost of reserving a flight. The company plans to expand beyond space tourism as well, to make travel on Earth more convenient. With the technology that the company is developing, they aim to be the only company that can take passengers at supersonic speed in a winged vehicle. With what the company calls "high speed global mobility vehicles," travel times across the globe could be drastically reduced. For example, it could become possible to travel from Tokyo to Los Angeles in just two hours. 30 35 40

While the possibility of space travel might seem to be something only for the very rich, the goal of these companies is to eventually bring these services to more and more people. New technologies become more affordable and more accessible over time. Perhaps it won't be long before space vacations become a common holiday choice. 45

COMPREHENSION
次の文を読み、本文の内容と合っていれば T、そうでない場合は F を選択しましょう。

1. There are already some companies with plans for tourism in space. [T / F]
2. Elon Musk has made a fortune from SpaceX's space trip. [T / F]
3. Yusaku Maezawa plans to invite more than eight artists to his trip to the moon. [T / F]
4. In 2018, Virgin Galactic was involved in an accident when its ship crashed and killed a pilot. [T / F]

MAKE A SUMMARY

内容に合うように下線部に適切な語句や文を入れ、要約を完成させましょう。

　　With the development of modern airline technology, we can go nearly anywhere <u>¹_____</u> manner and there will be opportunities for us to go into space for travel in the near future. SpaceX is planning 10-day space tours, but <u>²_____</u> <u>_____</u> with tickets costing $55 million. Yusaku Maezawa will be the first person to join a space tour to the moon, <u>³_____</u> <u>_____</u>. Virgin Galactic, regardless of its tragic accident in 2014, <u>⁴_____</u> <u>_____</u> in development. New technologies will make <u>⁵_____</u> over time. The day won't be long when space vacations are popular!

HAVE YOUR SAY

以下は "If you could afford to go on a space tour, would you go?" という問いに対する、ある学生の回答です。ペアを組み、下線部を自分たちに置き換えて、配布された記入用紙に書いてみましょう（その後、クラスで発表してみましょう）。

> If a space tour costs <u>up to 500,000 yen (about 5000 dollars)</u>, I would like to join one. I would like to <u>take a look at the earth from space</u>. Also I am really interested in <u>the life on other planets and I'd like to look for some clues</u>. However, I heard about <u>some accidents on spaceships recently</u> so if <u>my safety can't be guaranteed</u>, I'm not willing to go to space.

8 Gender and Sports

スポーツにおけるジェンダーを考える

ISTENING

TARGET!

様々な疑問文でいろいろな角度から質問してみましょう 🎧DL 51 ◉CD1-79

否定疑問文　**Aren't** you hungry? / **Can't** he come?

付加疑問文 （語尾のイントーネーションに注意）

　　You're tired, **aren't you**? / They don't know that, **do they**?

　　Open the window, **will you**? / Let's go, **shall we**?

関節疑問文 （語順に注意）

　　Tell me **why he is absent from school today**. / I don't know **what time it is now**.

選択疑問文　Would you like tea **or** coffee? — I'd like tea, please.

疑問詞を使った特殊な例

　　〈反語〉**Who** knows? / **Who** cares? →反語として「誰も～しないだろう」という意味を含む

　　〈What（無生物主語）＋使役動詞〉「なぜ～そうしたのか（何が～そうさせたのか）」

　　　　　　What brought you here? / **What made** you come to Japan?

WARM UP

🎧DL 52 ◉CD1-80

a ～ e の音声を聞き、1 ～ 5 の応答として適当なものをそれぞれ選びましょう。

1. Aren't you bored staying home all day?　　　　　（　　　）

2. Tell me which dress I should wear for the party.　（　　　）

3. Seems like it's going to rain soon, isn't it?　　　（　　　）

4. Would you like tea or coffee?　　　　　　　　　（　　　）

5. Why don't you come to the concert with us?　　　（　　　）

TRY LISTENING

🎧DL 53 ◉CD1-81

次は Emily のブログの抜粋です。これを聞き、（　　）に入る部分を補ってみましょう。

From Emily's blog

So angry with my brother Ben. He leaked to Mom my plan to study in Japan.
She asked me, "(　　　　　) on earth (　　　　) (　　　　) (　　　　　) of
this?" I told her that I wanted to study Japanese anime. Mom says it's too far
from here. (　　　　) (　　　　　　)? It is my life, (　　　　) (　　　　)?
Don't tell me (　　　　) (　　　　) (　　　　) (　　　　) or (　　　　)!

CONVERSATION

A. 次の会話を聞き、（　　）に適切な語を入れましょう。会話のあとに問題が流れるので、適切な答えを a、b から選びましょう。

Erina and Beth are talking on the way home from class.

Erina: Beth, you always look so good. ¹_____?

Beth: Thanks. Well, I work out a lot, just about every day. I'm very careful with what I eat. And I also practice martial arts.

Erina: Martial arts? Which one?

Beth: ²_____, judo and capoeira.

Erina: That's amazing. I know judo, but I don't know much about capoeira.

Beth: Capoeira is so fun! It combines dancing with fighting techniques. ³_____. Now, it's becoming popular worldwide.

Erina: I'd like to see you do it sometime! ⁴_____?

Beth: Well, I want to become a professional mixed martial arts fighter.

Erina: Seriously!? That's incredible!

Beth: Do you know Rena Nakagawa, the United Fighting Team star?

Erina: Of course! In fact, I saw her on TV just a few days ago.

Beth: She's always been my role model. Watching her inspires me and makes me feel like I can do it, too!

Erina: I think you can!

Beth: Really? ⁵_____!

Q1. **a.** It is a martial art aiming to raise professional martial arts fighters.
　　　b. It is a martial art which combines dancing and fighting techniques becoming known worldwide these days.

Q2. **a.** Because she wants to belong to the United Fighting Team in the future.
　　　b. Because she wants to become a professional mixed martial arts fighter.

B. クラスメートとペアを組み、完成した会話を発話練習してみましょう。

C. ▨▨▨部を参考に、同じペアで次の①または②のシチュエーションで会話をしてみましょう。

① ボルダリングをすること（bouldering）は私に活力を与え、どんな困難も乗り越えられるような気にもさせる。

② １日２回コーヒーを飲むことは兄に活力を与え、20 代でいるような気にもさせた。

52

SHORT ANNOUNCEMENT

🎧 DL 55 💿 CD1-83

A. 次のラジオ番組の抜粋を聞き、下線部に適切な語句を入れましょう。

Welcome, everyone, to our weekly spotlight on influential athletes. Today we are going to talk about the incredible fighter, Rena Nakagawa. In a rough sport [1]_____, Rena has emerged as one of the biggest stars in mixed martial arts. Since her debut in 2015, Rena's career has skyrocketed. In 2017 she became [2]_____ _____ the United Fighting Team. Six months later she was the first woman to appear on the cover of the magazine *Fantastic Fight*. In 2018, Rena entered the world of professional wrestling. She quickly rose to the top and is now the first woman ever to have won both mixed martial arts and wrestling championships. She has also headlined several pay-per-view events. Rena's influence [3]_____, as well. She has appeared on several TV shows and does regular modeling work. Recently, she has proven to be talented at acting and has starred in several major films. What a remarkable human being!

B. 次の文がメッセージの内容に合致している場合は T、そうでない場合は F を選択しましょう。

1. Most of the mixed martial arts fighters are male.   [T / F]
2. Rena Nakagawa won two championships before she became a professional wrestler.   [T / F]
3. She has just turned her talents to working as a TV and movie star recently.

[T / F]

C. ペアを組み、____部を参考に次のような女性の特徴をアナウンスしてみましょう。必要に応じて自分たちで情報を付け加えて話しましょう。

> ・彼女は女性で初めてエベレスト (Mt. Everest) 登頂に成功した登山家 (mountaineer) です。
> ・イタリア料理のシェフをしながら、オペラ歌手 (opera singer) の活動もしています。

READING

いろいろな受動態の用法を理解しましょう

助動詞と受動態　That used car **may be bought** by my brother.

進行形と受動態　All the computers **are being used** by the students.

現在完了形と受動態
　I **have been helped** many times by her. 「彼女には何度も助けられた」＝経験

受動態を用いる慣用表現：
　be born 「生まれる」　*be* married 「結婚している」　*be* injured 「怪我をする」
　be surprised at ~ 「〜に驚く」　*be* pleased with ~ 「〜が気に入る」
　be covered with ~ 「〜で覆われている」　*be* satisfied with ~ 「〜に満足する」
　be disappointed at ~ 「〜に失望する」　*be* known to ~ 「〜で知られている」

GRAMMAR EXERCISE 1

日本語を参考に〔　　〕内の語句を並べ替えて文を完成させましょう。

1. 私は自分の健康のために禁煙するよう命じられています。

[my / ordered / refrain / have / been / I / smoking / to / from / for / health].

_____

2. アレックスはバドミントンを練習中にひどい怪我をした。

[practicing / was / Alex / when / injured / badminton / badly].

_____

3. たくさんの人に見られるのには慣れていません。

[used / people / watched / not / to / being / by / I'm / so many].

_____

GRAMMAR EXERCISE 2

日本語の意味になるように文を作ってみましょう。

1. すべての食器は厚いほこりに覆われていた。

_____

2. 彼らは結婚して 24 年になり、5 人の子供がいます。

_____

DEFINITION FOR READING
1～5の語句の定義として正しいものをa～eから選んでみましょう。

1. empower (*l.*8) _____   **a.** the giving of public support to an idea or action

2. platform (*l.*10) _____   **b.** the act of giving up your job or position

3. advocacy (*l.*16) _____   **c.** an opportunity to express your ideas to people

4. resignation (*l.*24) _____   **d.** feeling that you are sorry for doing something wrong

5. apologetic (*l.*29) _____   **e.** to give someone more control over their situation

READING
 DL 56 CD1-84 ～ CD1-88

次の文章を読み、あとに続く問題に答えましょう。

Gender Equality in Sports

One of the most important human rights issues that modern society faces is that of gender equality. And the field of sports is one place where progress is being made. Athletics offers a powerful means for social change and for bringing people together of different races, nationalities and genders. While equality in sport has come a long way, there is still much work to be done.   5

The International Olympic Committee (IOC) is one organization at the forefront of the movement to empower women in sports. In the words of Thomas Bach, the president of the IOC, "I firmly believe that sport is one of the most powerful platforms for promoting gender equality and empowering   10 women and girls." The IOC has initiated the Gender Equality Review Project, which outlines 25 recommendations for making the Olympics more gender equal. Also, in the IOC Olympic Agenda 2020, the IOC calls for increasing female participation at the Olympic Games to 50 percent. The IOC has also recommended more female officials, coaches and heads of commissions.   15

Advocacy for gender equality in sports is being taken up by different organizations around the world. For example, in 2020, the first summit of its kind was held in Belize to promote equality for women and girls involved in sports. There has been a decline in the number of women engaged in sports in Belize. According to the summit organizers, there is a lack of opportunities for women   20 wanting to play sports, as well as a lack of support from people in power.

55

Recently, Carlos Cordeiro resigned as president of the U.S. Soccer Federation (USSF). The resignation came after the organization sparked public outrage when it's legal papers in a gender discrimination lawsuit claimed the women's national team had less responsibility and physical ability than the men's team. The women's national team was suing the organization because they claimed they were not paid equally to the men's national team. Cordeiro was apologetic and, concerning his resignation, wrote, "It has become clear to me that what is best right now is a new direction." Regarding the wording in the legal papers, he wrote, "The arguments and language… caused great offense and pain, especially to our extraordinary women's national team players who deserve better. It was unacceptable and inexcusable." Afterwards, Cindy Parlow, a former midfielder, was elected as the first woman president in the 107-year history of the USSF.

While it has been making an effort, Japan is still behind with gender equality in sports. In 2017, five major Japanese sports organizations signed the Brighton Plus Helsinki 2014 Declaration on Women & Sport, an international statement advocating the empowerment of women in sports. However, a photo taken just after the signing of the statement shows five men who signed the document standing in the front row while women who worked hard in support of the signing were put at the rear. Some have said this shows the reality of gender equality in the Japanese Sports Community. A survey conducted by the Japanese Sports Association in October 2018 showed that women accounted for only 11.2 percent of the board members in 117 sports organizations across Japan. While there has been significant progress in recent years, much more needs to be done in support of women in athletic communities throughout the world.

COMPREHENSION

次の文を読み、本文の内容と合っていれば T、そうでない場合は F を選択しましょう。

1. The Gender Equality Review Project aims to make Olympic participation equal for men and women. [T / F]

2. The IOC Olympic Agenda 2020 requests more than 40% of female
   participants at the Olympic games. [T / F]
3. Carlos Cordeiro resigned because of gender discrimination against the U.S.
   women's national soccer team. [T / F]
4. The survey in 2018 shows that more than 20% of board members of sports
   organizations in Japan are women. [T / F]

MAKE A SUMMARY
DL 57   CD1-89

内容に合うように下線部に適切な語句や文を入れ、要約を完成させましょう。

　　Gender equality in sports is an important issue in the modern society,
however, still much work has to be done. The IOC has initiated a project in
which they recommend making the Olympics more ¹_____
and called for increasing ²_____. On the other
hand, discriminatory behaviors against women forced Carlos Cordeiro
to resign as president of the USSF and Cindy Parlow was elected as the
first woman president. In Japan, some major companies have declared
to ³_____ of women in sports, but the reality
shows that ⁴_____. Much more needs to
be done in support of women ⁵_____.

HAVE YOUR SAY

以下は "How can we get into exercising regularly?" という問いに対するある学
生の回答です。ペアを組み、これを自分たちに置き換えて、下線部を書き換えてみま
しょう（その後、クラスで発表してみましょう）。

　　Everyone knows that exercise is good for us to improve our
health, however, it tends to be hard to implement it regularly in
the long term. There are some suggestions for everyone to get
involved in exercise. For example, start with something simple that
you can keep up for at least two weeks such as walking for 30
minutes. Also, have goals that are easy to achieve such as light
stretching. These may be small things, but adding them up every
day will lead to a big result.

9 New "Old" Entertainment

懐かしいエンタメを新発見！

ISTENING

TARGET!

話者の意見・主張が何かを理解しましょう　🎧 DL 58　◎ CD2-02

意見や主張をする際に使う表現

〈動詞〉

考えや意見を述べる　（一般的）think　（推測）guess, suppose
　　　　　　　　　　（強い意見や主張）believe, argue, claim, maintain

肯定する、好意的に思う　support, agree, favor, accept, approve of, like, prefer

否定する、批判する　object, oppose, disagree, be against, resist, disapprove of,
　　　　　　　　　　dislike

主張をぼかす、言わない　be not sure / don't(doesn't) know / maybe / have no idea

〈その他の表現〉

　（理由を述べるとき）The reason is... / because, since, as / due to... /（理由に続けて）
　　　　　　　　　　　That's why...

　（個人的見解を述べるとき）In my opinion... / In my case... / Personally...

　（意見・主張を切り出すとき）Frankly... / Clearly...

　（まとめの見解を述べるとき）To recap... / To sum up... / Finally... / Eventually...

WARM UP　🎧 DL 59　◎ CD2-03

次の1〜5が肯定的であればPを、否定的であればNを選択してみましょう。

1. [P / N]　　　**2.** [P / N]　　　**3.** [P / N]　　　**4.** [P / N]　　　**5.** [P / N]

TRY LISTENING　🎧 DL 60　◎ CD2-04

次は "Which do you like better, eating out or eating at home?" という問いか
けに対する5人の男女の回答です。これを聞いて、外食派と家食派、どっちつかず派
に5人を仕分けしてみましょう。

　外食派　　　［　　　　　　　　　　　　　　　　　　　　　］

　家食派　　　［　　　　　　　　　　　　　　　　　　　　　］

　どっちつかず派　　［　　　　　　　　　　　　　　　　　　　　　］

　回答者　　| Kate　Julie　Miki　Don　Owen |

CONVERSATION

DL 61 · CD2-05

A. 次の会話を聞き、（　）に適切な語を入れましょう。会話のあとに問題が流れるので、適切な答えを a、b から選びましょう。

Beth comes to Paul's room while he and Brandon are relaxing.

Beth: Hi guys! That music sounds so good! Who is it?

Paul: That's Shelly Love, she's one of my favorite artists. But that's not the only reason it sounds good; it's a vinyl album, not a CD or MP3.
1 _____.

Brandon: I don't know, digital music sounds just as good to me.
And 2 _____!

Paul: No way, 3 _____!

Beth: Well, I stopped by to see if you wanted to go see the new film *A Future Time*. Have you seen it?
4 _____.

Paul: Not yet. Isn't that filmed on 70mm? I heard the director wanted to make a film that reminded people of the old classics.

Brandon: Well, if so, I'm sure Paul will want to see it, since it uses old technology!

Paul: That's right. I'd love to go. 70mm is
5 _____.

Beth: Great! The show starts at 6:00 PM.

Q1. a. Brandon believes 70mm film is much better than modern digital film.
b. Paul is in favor of listening to music and watching films that use old technology.

Q2. a. Because it can be easily stored.
b. Because he can easily access the music online.

B. クラスメートとペアを組み、完成した会話を発話練習してみましょう。

C. ＿＿部を参考に、同じペアで次の①または②のシチュエーションで互いに発話してみましょう。

① 彼の父は、家族に昔の日々を思い出させる家を建てたかった。

② 昨日、私は元カノを思い出させる人に出会った。

SHORT ANNOUNCEMENT

A. 次のラジオ番組を聞き、下線部に適切な語句を入れましょう。

Hello everyone and welcome to my weekly movie review. Here I talk about the latest must-see films for all movie buffs out there. I have just got back from seeing the *A Future Time* and I can tell you, it is fantastic. ¹ _____,
this film combines a futuristic sci-fi world with an intriguing story and characters that are both contemporary and believable. But perhaps ² _____,
on classic 70mm film, the same kind that was used when I was a kid. ³ _____. I highly recommend *A Future Time* to anyone looking for an exciting way to pass a few hours. And definitely try and catch it in a theater that has 70mm projectors. You'll be glad you did!

B. 次の文がメッセージの内容に合致している場合は T、そうでない場合は F を選択しましょう。

1. *A Future Time* is a wonderful romantic comedy.　　　　　　　[T / F]

2. The speaker saw the film when he was a kid.　　　　　　　　[T / F]

3. It is recommended to see this film at a theater with 70mm projectors.

　　　　　　　　　　　　　　　　　　　　　　　　　　　　[T / F]

C. ペアを組み、▢▢部を参考にオックスフォードの感想と、同地滞在をペアにお勧めしてみましょう。必要に応じて自分たちで情報を付け加えて話しましょう。

> ・たった今オックフォードから戻ってきたばかりですが、はっきり言って、言葉になりません。
> ・美しい川の流れ（waterways）や自然を求める人はオックスフォードに滞在することを強く勧めます。

EADING

TARGET!

様々な完了形の違いを理解し、使いこなしましょう

```
         過去まで          過去から現在まで        現在から未来まで
    ·········▶          ·········▶          ·········▶
   ||||||||||||| 過去 ||||||||||||| 現在 |||||||||||| 未来
     （過去完了）          （現在完了）           （未来完了）
```

1. 現在完了〈**have [has]** + **過去分詞**〉＝現在までの完了・経験・継続する動作・状態
   I **have known** him since he was eight years old. →継続する状態

2. 過去完了〈**had** + **過去分詞**〉＝過去のある時点までの完了・経験・継続する動作・状態
   They **had been** searching for five months when their parrot was found. →継続する状態

3. 未来完了〈**will**+ **have**+ **過去分詞**〉＝未来のある時までの完了・経験・継続する動作・状態
   The sun **will have risen** by seven o'clock tomorrow. →完了

GRAMMAR EXERCISE 1

日本語の意味になるように（　　）に適切な語を記入しましょう。

1. 大学を終えるときにあなたは 10 年間英語を勉強したことになる。

You (　　　　) (　　　　) (　　　　　　) English for 10 years

(　　　　) the (　　　　) you finish university.

2. あなたのアカウントは不正なログイン操作が複数回あったのでロックされています。

Your account (　　　　) (　　　　) (　　　　　) due to multiple failed

login attempts.

3. トーマスが教室に入るやいなや、彼は異変に気づいた。

Hardly (　　　　) Thomas (　　　　　) the classroom (　　　　) he

noticed something was wrong.

GRAMMAR EXERCISE 2

日本語の意味になるように文を作ってみましょう。

1. あなたのガンは 5 年以内に完全に除去されていることでしょう。

_____

2. アメリカに行く前は、ネイティブの英語話者と話したことがなかった。

_____

DEFINITION FOR READING

1 〜 5 の語句の定義として正しいものを a 〜 e から選んでみましょう。

1. renaissance (*l.*5) _____
2. remarkable (*l.*11) _____
3. authenticity (*l.*23) _____
4. accomplish (*l.*33) _____
5. apex (*l.*36) _____

a. to succeed in doing or completing something
b. a new interest in something, especially a particular subject, or form of art
c. the top or highest part of something
d. unusual or surprising in a way that causes people to take notice
e. the quality of being genuine or true

READING

次の文章を読み、あとに続く問題に答えましょう。

The Return of 70mm Film

Though there have been many modern technological advances, some people prefer the old ways, for example, vinyl instead of MP3 or books instead of digital readers. With film, too, many fans and movie makers prefer classic methods to contemporary ones. One type of movie making, in particular, that

5　has seen a renaissance recently, is the use of 70mm film instead of digital.

A type of analog film, 70mm film has been around for a very long time. In fact, some classic movies such as *Ben-Hur* or *Lawrence of Arabia* were shot on 70mm film. With this kind of film, the frames on the reel are 70mm in width. Normally, the frames are 35mm and movies are still enjoyable to

10　watch. But the difference in visual quality with using 70mm film is quite remarkable. This type of film changes the aspect ratio of the film image, as well, making movies shot in 70mm ideal for large, wide theater screens. IMAX films are also shot on a special type of 70mm film.

In contrast to 70mm film, digital film is recorded as digital video

15　images. Digital film uses light sensors and digital receptors to capture images similar to digital photographs. There are various levels of resolution with digital film, ranging from high definition video through 4K and now

20　even 8K. One might think that digital film is far better than 70mm analog film, but that is

not the case. The two types of films are actually relatively comparable. There is also a sense of authenticity and a classic feel to watching films in 70mm.

Quentin Tarantino, the well-known movie director and producer, has made a lot of effort to bring the 70mm experience to modern audiences. He shot his film *The Hateful Eight,* entirely on a type of high quality 70mm film called Ultra Panavision. He also used customized anamorphic lenses to create a spectacular wide-screen experience. In order for people to experience the full visual quality of this type of movie, Tarantino installed custom movie projectors in to 100 movies theaters across America. As a result, Steve Bellamy, the president of the Kodak film company, wrote a letter of thanks to Tarantino. Bellamy wrote, "We at Kodak would like to take a moment to recognize what the Tarantino team accomplished with *The Hateful Eight* as it was more than just making a movie on the gold standard of film, or a preservation of the past. They did not just create the analog of analog, but they created a new apex for analog."

Other well-known film makers such as Steven Spielberg and J.J. Abrams have also used 70mm film. In fact many modern hits, such as *Rogue One: A Star Wars Story* and *Wonder Woman*, have been shot on 70mm. Both digital and 70mm have their benefits, and as to which one is better, it largely comes down to personal preference. But the fact that some very talented movie makers continue to use the 70mm medium gives moviegoers an exciting and nostalgic option in what they choose for entertainment.

note: **anamorphic** (*l.*27)「アナモフィック・レンズを使った、シネマスコープの」(35mm フィルムの縦横比 ＝約３対４よりずっと横幅が広い画角で撮影されたもので、この方式の商標名「シネマスコープ」でよく知られる)

COMPREHENSION

次の文を読み、本文の内容と合っていれば T、そうでない場合は F を選択しましょう。

1. Nowadays most films are shot on 35 or 70mm films. [T / F]

2. Digital film is better than analog film in quality and authenticity. [T / F]

3. Bellamy installed custom projectors in to 100 movie theaters in America.

[T / F]

4. Tarantino gave opportunities to modern audience to experience 70mm film.

[T / F]

MAKE A SUMMARY

DL 64 · CD2-12

内容に合うように下線部に適切な語句や文を入れ、要約を完成させましょう。

　　70mm analog film ¹＿＿＿＿＿＿＿＿＿＿＿ for a long time, and filmmakers are beginning to recognize its value again. Especially it is ²＿＿＿＿＿＿＿＿＿＿＿＿＿. On the other hand, digital film is recorded as digital video images. Digital film uses light sensors and digital receptors ³＿＿＿＿＿＿＿＿＿＿＿＿. One might think that digital film is far better than 70mm analog film but ⁴＿＿＿＿＿＿＿＿＿. Quentin Tarantino had made efforts to bring the 70mm experience to the modern audience. He used customized anamorphic lenses to create a spectacular wide-screen experience. Both digital and 70mm have their benefits, and as to which is better, it ⁵＿＿＿＿＿＿＿＿＿＿.

HAVE YOUR SAY

以下は "Which do you prefer, digital or analog?" という問いに対するある学生の回答です。ペアを組み、これを自分たちに置き換えて、下線部を書き換えてみましょう（その後、クラスで発表してみましょう）。

> 　　I prefer <u>digital</u> to <u>analog</u>, because <u>digital data is easy to recognize</u>. For example, <u>when I weigh myself by a digital scale, I can see my weight quite accurately</u>. In addition, <u>some electronic thermometer can take a temperature without touching someone's body</u>. But when it comes to <u>listening to music</u>, it is often said that <u>digital sound is inferior to the sound made by analog devices</u>. However, I prefer to use <u>digital devices in my everyday life</u>, since they are very convenient.

New Way to Enjoy Cinema

···

映画は劇場派？ おうち派？

LISTENING

グラフィックと照合して情報を聞き取りましょう 🎧 DL 65 ◉ CD2-13

絵や写真、図などのグラフィック情報と照合して英語を聞き取るときのコツ

1. 位置関係を把握する→前置詞に着目

under / above / on / between / next to / across / opposite など

2.（人物の）動作や表情を把握する→進行形・形容詞に着目

［動作］An old man **is standing** in the middle of the road.

［表情］Deborah's face turned **pale** on hearing the news.

3. 図・グラフで数の推移や数の比較を把握する→動詞・比較表現に着目

［推移］（上昇・増加）be (go) up / rise / soar / elevate / boost / surge / increase

（下降・減少）be (go) down / lower / slip / decrease / decline

［数の比較］Last year's average oil price **is much higher than** this year's.

History class starts **the earliest of** the three.

WARM UP 🎧 DL 66 ◉ CD2-14

次の A、B についてそれぞれ 2 つの文が読まれます。各文につき、内容と合致するものは T、そうでないものは F を選びましょう。

A

1. [T / F]
2. [T / F]

B

1. [T / F]
2. [T / F]

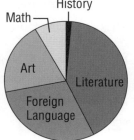

Favorite Subject

Math — History — Art — Literature — Foreign Language

TRY LISTENING 🎧 DL 67 ◉ CD2-15

Josh が自分の部屋を説明した音声を聞き、以下の見取り図の A ～ D に相当するものを記入してみましょう。

Josh's Room

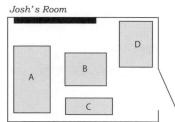

A (　　　　　　　　　)

B (　　　　　　　　　)

C (　　　　　　　　　)

D (　　　　　　　　　)

CONVERSATION

DL 68 · CD2-16

A. 次の会話を聞き、（　　）に適切な語を入れましょう。会話のあとに問題が流れるので、適切な答えを a 〜 c から選びましょう。

Three students are talking about what to do tonight.

Erina: What do you guys feel like doing tonight? How about going out to a movie?

Brandon: That sounds good. I heard that World Cinemas remodeled their theater and the seats ¹_____ now.

Paul: Why don't we just stay home and watch some videos on Netflix? It's easier.

Brandon: That could be fun, too. Also, ²_____ .

Erina: Oh, come on, guys. ³_____ . Besides, movies are much more fun to watch in the theater.

Paul: Really? I don't know. Watching from home, we can talk with each other and don't have to worry about disturbing others. Also, ⁴_____ .

Erina: Yes, but at the theater, they've got an amazing sound system, ⁵_____ _____ IMAX and 3D movies.

Brandon: Well, you guys both have good points, but doesn't World Cinemas have new gourmet popcorn flavors?

Paul: Oh, that's right! OK, fine! Let's go!

Q1. **a.** It is cheaper.
b. We can control the video as we like.
c. No need to worry about our noise level.

Q2. **a.** IMAX and 3D system **b.** nicer seats **c.** popcorn

B. クラスメートとペアを組み、完成した会話を発話練習してみましょう。

C. ▓▓部を参考に、同じペアで次の①または②のシチュエーションで会話をしてみましょう。

① 今夜、外へ夕食を食べに行こうと提案する。

② コーヒーでも飲みながらその件（問題）について議論しようと提案する。

SHORT ANNOUNCEMENT 🎧 DL 69   ◎ CD2-17

A. 次の宣伝メッセージの抜粋を聞き、下線部に適切な語句を入れましょう。

Looking to have a fun night out? Here at World Cinemas, we have completely redesigned your movie viewing experience. Along with our fantastic new food menu, we now feature three improved seating options. Standard seats are located ¹ _____ and feature additional legroom and wider armrests. Deluxe seats are ² _____ the cinema and feature spacious, plush leather seats and a small table by each seat. And, if you are looking for a truly luxurious experience, we invite you to try our Premium seats. Our 14 Premium seats are located on a raised floor ³ _____ .

Each of these lavish reclining seats features an adjustable leg-rest and comes with a private table and coatrack. The Premium floor is accessed by an entrance through our Premium lounge. In the lounge, you can relax and enjoy some of our gourmet food offerings before the show. Whatever your preference, we are ready to provide you with a movie experience like no other!

B. メッセージの内容に合致するように、座席表のA～Cが以下のどのシートに該当するかを選んでみましょう。

1. Premium   (   )
2. Standard   (   )
3. Deluxe   (   )

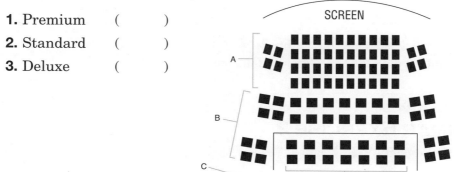

C. ペアを組み、▨▨部を参考に次のようなメキシカンレストランの特徴をアナウンスしてみましょう。必要に応じて自分たちで情報を付け加えて話しましょう。

> ・伝統のメキシコ料理に加え、たくさんの当店オリジナルメニューを特徴にしました。
> ・未知の激辛体験をお求めなら、当店のハバネロ・チリ（Habanero Chili）を試してみることをお勧めします。

READING

不定詞・動名詞の基本とその違いを学びましょう

1. to 不定詞＝「to+ 動詞の原形」で名詞・形容詞・副詞の働きをする
名詞的用法「〜すること」・形容詞的用法「〜するための」・副詞的用法「〜するために」
His grandmother needs someone **to take** care of her.

2. 動名詞＝「動詞の -ing」で名詞の働きをする。主語、目的語、補語になる
After a pause, Olivia started **talking** about her spooky campfire story.

3. to 不定詞と動名詞のニュアンスの違い
I tried **to go** to the theater last night, but I could not go out.

→未来や実現しなかった出来事

I tried **going** to the theater last night, but it was closed. →現実や実現した出来事

GRAMMAR EXERCISE 1
日本語を参考に［　　］内の語句を並べ替えて、文を完成させましょう。

1. その会社は今年、30 店舗をオープンさせることを予定している。
[year / stores / company / to / the / expects / open / 30 / this].

_____

2. どうしたらあのような同じ間違いをしないようにできますか。
[mistake / avoid / can / same / how / I / making / that]?

_____

3. ジェシカは最善を尽くしたが、また失敗した。
[best, / did / again / to / her / Jessica / fail / only].

_____

GRAMMAR EXERCISE 2
日本語の意味になるように文を作ってみましょう。

1. その劇場は新しいスタッフを雇う余裕がなかった。

_____

2. 私はその画家の自伝を以前に買ったことを忘れていた。

_____

DEFINITION FOR READING

1〜5の語句の定義として正しいものをa〜eから選んでみましょう。

1. upsurge (*l*.1) _____   **a.** original, not resembling something previously known

2. extinction (*l*.3) _____   **b.** something that is provided for other people

3. novel (*l*.15) _____   **c.** a sudden rise or large increase

4. entice (*l*.8) _____   **d.** a situation in which a way of life stops existing

5. offering (*l*.15) _____   **e.** to persuade someone to do something

READING

 DL 70   CD2-18 〜 CD2-22

次の文章を読み、あとに続く問題に答えましょう。

The Changing Face of Cinemas

With the upsurge of online streaming services, movie theaters are being forced to change the way they do business. It is becoming vital that cinemas adapt to new customer expectations or they may face extinction. While there are many ways that they are doing this, two methods have been particularly successful. Movie theaters have begun improving their facilities 　5 and offering subscription services.

Some theaters now offer full course restaurant services as well as deluxe reclining seats for viewers in an effort to entice customers away from their streaming devices at home. For example, in some of its theaters in Japan, the movie chain 109 Cinemas offers private lounges and restrooms 　10 for its deluxe-seat customers. Customers can also order from gourmet menus and have their food brought directly to them by servers as they are watching films. These extra services make watching films in theaters a very different experience from watching them at home.

One novel strategy that is becoming popular is the offering of 　15 subscriptions to movie theaters. Cinemas are competing with SVOD (subscription video on demand) services by becoming more like SVOD services. Some theater chains in the USA have adopted a subscription plan of some kind, and the result has been an increase in moviegoers. For example, AMC, the largest movie chain in the USA, has a subscription plan where 　20 customers can see up to three movies per week in both 3-D and IMAX for $20.00 to $24.00 a month, depending on location. There is an app available so subscribers can select the show time and seating from their mobile device. After the first year of service, AMC had 860,000 subscribers, far more than the 500,000 they had originally expected.

While SVOD services have put pressure on movie theaters to upgrade their offerings to entertainment seekers, there is also evidence that suggests streaming services do not negatively impact movie attendance. A research firm recently surveyed moviegoers and found that SVOD users who reported watching 13 or more movies in the past 12 months saw on average 6.5 movies in theaters. Customers who watched 1 to 12 movies via streaming services saw an average of 5.2 movies in theaters and those who didn't watch any movies via SVOD saw an average of 5.3 movies in theaters over the past 12 months. This data shows that those people who watch a lot of movies online also seem to attend movie theaters frequently. And there isn't much difference in the theater attendance rates between those who use SVOD service less frequently and those who don't use SVOD services at all.

These changes that movie theaters are making are significant steps in ensuring that cinemas survive into the future. While it is possible to imagine a world where people no longer need to visit cinemas, surely there is a place for movie theaters as society evolves. Going out to the movies is a precious experience that seems to only be getting better.

COMPREHENSION

次の文を読み、本文の内容と合っていれば T、そうでない場合は F を選択しましょう。

1. This passage concludes that it's better to watch movies online at home.

[T / F]

2. Watching films in theaters is becoming a special experience today.   [T / F]

3. Subscribers of movie theaters can select show times and seating options by
   mobile apps.   [T / F]
4. Research shows the number of moviegoers has decreased a lot due to SVOD
   services.   [T / F]

MAKE A SUMMARY   DL 71   CD2-23

内容に合うように下線部に適切な語句や文を入れ、要約を完成させましょう。

　　Movie theaters are changing the way they do business. They are improving
their facilities and ¹_____. With luxurious
seating options and services, watching films in theaters ²_____
_____ from watching at home. Also, subscription
services are increasing ³_____. For
example, AMC has 860,000 subscribers, which is far more than they had
originally expected. Though SVOD services are seen as ⁴_____
_____, they actually do not negatively impact movie
attendance. Movie theaters are changing to ensure that ⁵_____
_____.

HAVE YOUR SAY

以下は "Which do you prefer, watching films in movie theaters or at home?"
という問いに対するある学生の回答です。ペアを組み、これを自分たちに置き換えて、
下線部を書き換えてみましょう（その後、クラスで発表してみましょう）。

> 　　I like watching films in movie theaters. There are two reasons.
> First, it is a good opportunity to go out and spend time with my
> friends. Not only watching the movie itself, but having time with
> them at cafés or restaurants in theaters is fun. Second, we can
> talk about the cinemas after leaving the movie theater. This is also
> quite interesting. In short, I like watching movies in theaters rather
> than at home.

Unit

11 Fbake Meat or No Meat?

フェイクミートは肉の代替となる？

ISTENING

TARGET!

チャンクリスニングのコツを覚えましょう 🎧 DL 72 ◎ CD2-24

チャンク（意味のかたまり）で聞く訓練をすることで、内容の理解がしやすくなります。
When I was doing / homework, / my mother / brought me / some snacks / that I
ate immediately.
私がしているとき／宿題を／母が／私に買ってくれた／軽食を／私はすぐに食べた

意味が理解できない場合はスキップして次のチャンクの理解に集中するようにします。
US senator Martha McSally, / a Republican from Arizona, / is asking Congress /
to extend the $600 per week expansion / to unemployment insurance / for one
week...						(*The Guardian*, 2020.7.30)
アメリカ上院議員マーサ・マクサリーは／アリゾナ州選出の共和党員で／議会に求めてい
る／週600ドル増額の延長を／失業保険（給付）の／あと一週間

WARM UP 🎧 DL 73 ◎ CD2-25

次の音声をチャンクごとに聞き、（　　）に適語を入れて各チャンクの意味を完成さ
せましょう。

1. 私たちが（　　　　　　　）とき／私たちは（　　　　　　　）ものだ／
毎（　　　　　）／私たちは（　　　　　　）／（　　　　　　）の近くに／
そして川で（　　　　　　　）／また（　　　　　　　　）／
（　　　　　　）のために
2. （　　　　　　　　　）は／（　　　　　　　　　）した／
（　　　　　　）を（　　　　　　　）することについて／
（　　　　　　）を通じて／（　　　　　　）の中に

TRY LISTENING 🎧 DL 74 ◎ CD2-26

次の文を聞き、1〜6についての情報を記入しましょう。

1. いつ？（　　　　　　　　　）　　2. 誰が？（　　　　　　　　　）
3. どうした？（　　　　　　　）　　4. 誰と？（　　　　　　　　　）
5. the Quarrymen とは？（　　　　　　　　　　）
6. Liverpool Institute とは？（　　　　　　　　　　）

72

CONVERSATION

 DL 75 CD2-27

A. 次の会話を聞き、（　　）に適切な語を入れましょう。会話のあとに問題が流れるので、適切な答えを a ～ c から選びましょう。

Beth met Erina and Paul for the first time in weeks.

Beth: You guys both look so healthy! How did you lose weight?

Erina: We became vegetarians. It was hard at first but now we really enjoy it.

Beth: So, you don't eat any meat at all? What about stuff like eggs and cheese?

Erina: I still eat eggs and dairy, but I ¹_____ _____. It's delicious but so fattening!

Paul: I'm a vegan, so I don't eat any animal products at all. ²_____, I've felt great!

Beth: ³_____. I've been eating so much junk lately. But it seems so hard to become a vegetarian. I love food too much!

Erina: There are plenty of great vegetarian dishes. Trust me!

Paul: You could start by just giving up red meat. Cut out beef and pork and ⁴_____. Then you could start cutting out other kinds of meat.

Beth: But I love meat!

Paul: Well, if you really miss meat, ⁵_____ _____ now. They taste like meat but are much healthier.

Beth: Hmm. I really do need to do something. Maybe I should give it a try.

Q1. **a.** eggs **b.** cheese **c.** meat

Q2 **a.** stop eating all meat **b.** start cutting red meat **c.** try meat substitutes

B. クラスメートとペアを組み、完成した会話を発話練習してみましょう。

C. ▭部を参考に、同じペアで次の①または②のシチュエーションで会話をしてみましょう。

① どうやって痩せたかを聞く →（答え）一ヶ月前からジョギングを毎朝している。最初、朝起きるのはつらかったが、今はとても楽しんでいる。

② どうやってそのソフトの使い方を学んだかを聞く →（答え）コンピューターに詳しい兄がいて、彼に教えてもらった。最初、コンピューター言語を理解するのは大変だったが、今は楽しんで使っている。

SHORT ANNOUNCEMENT

A. 次のスピーチを聞き、下線部に適切な語句を入れましょう。

Hello everyone. Thank you for joining us today. While being a vegetarian is not for everyone, I know those of you in the audience today are interested in making the change but find it difficult. Well, I'm here to tell you that it's easier than you think. First, you need a good reason. If you become a vegetarian just for fun, you probably [1]_____ _____. Think about why you want to move to a plant-based diet. Next, you'll need to find good recipes. There is an abundance of websites devoted to great vegetarian cooking. Try one new recipe a week and eventually [2]_____ _____. Also, don't feel you have to give everything up at once. Start with red meat and gradually work towards abstaining from other kinds of meat. There are also fake meat products to help [3]_____.
It won't be long before you don't even miss meat!

B. 次の文がメッセージの内容に合致している場合はT、そうでない場合はFを選択しましょう。

1. It's possible to keep a vegetarian diet if your motive is just for fun. [T / F]
2. Speaker recommends to try a new recipe weekly and then you'll find some that you really love. [T / F]
3. If you suffer from a craving for meat, fake meat is an option. [T / F]

C. ペアを組み、上記のスピーチ文をチャンクごとに／（スラッシュ）で区切り、チャンクを意識しながら声に出して読んでみましょう。

READING

TARGET!

いろいろな接続詞や接続副詞を使いこなしましょう

1. 時を表すもの   when, while, as, after, before, until など
   He didn't say a word **until** the classroom became quiet.

2. 条件を表すもの   if, unless, although, though など
   She'll go broke **unless** she stops wasting money now.

3. 理由を表すもの   because, so, therefore, since, as など
   I am a vegan **so** I cannot eat meat. / I'm a student **therefore** I study hard.

4. 反意・対立を表すもの   but, however, nevertheless, yet, still など
   The book was very interesting, **however** it didn't sell well.

5. 並立・添加を表すもの   and, also, moreover, furthermore, besides など
   We ordered chicken nuggets. **Also,** we had hamburgers.

6. 対比・選択   or, while, otherwise, whether など
   I'll leave by noon, **otherwise** I'll miss my flight.

GRAMMAR EXERCISE 1

（　　　）に入る語を語群から選んで文を完成させましょう。

1. Even (　　　　　　) she didn't mean to hurt my feelings, I'll never forgive her.

2. Jake is four years younger, (　　　　　　) he is my brother's best friend.

3. The doctor recommended he be admitted to the hospital immediately, (　　　　　　) he continued shooting the film.

4. We should skip some steps. (　　　　　　), this project won't be finished by the end of the year.

5. It's hard to resist our chicken chili (　　　　) you're not a fan of spicy meals.

語群　　besides   unless   though   nevertheless   otherwise

GRAMMAR EXERCISE 2

日本語の意味になるように文を作ってみましょう。

1. 日本では電子書籍の売り上げが伸びた一方、ほかのアジア諸国では減少した。

_____

2. 会議を行うかどうかは、明日の調査の結果しだいだ。

_____

DEFINITION FOR READING

1 〜 5 の語句の定義として正しいものを a 〜 e から選んでみましょう。

1. livestock (*l*.4)   ____   **a.** a thick, soft paste

2. poultry (*l*.7)   ____   **b.** having or showing no moral principles

3. texture (*l*.23)   ____   **c.** the feel or appearance of a substance

4. mush (*l*.26)   ____   **d.** fowl raised for eggs or meat

5. unscrupulous (*l*.35)   ____   **e.** farm animals

READING

DL 77   CD2-29 〜 CD2-33

次の文章を読み、あとに続く問題に答えましょう。

Fake Meat is Fake Health?

These days more and more people are choosing to become vegetarians. The reasons why are many. Some people want to improve their health or lose weight. Others might do so for religious reasons or because they are concerned about the use of hormones or chemicals in livestock. Some people even choose

5   to become vegetarians because it is a cheaper way to live.

There are different kinds of vegetarianism, of course. For example, lacto-ovo vegetarians do not eat any fish, meat or poultry but eat eggs and dairy products. Lacto vegetarians are similar except they include eggs in the foods they don't eat, consuming only plant-based foods and dairy products.

10   Vegans don't eat any animal products whatsoever, restricting their diet purely to plant-based products. Regardless of the reasons or type of vegetarianism, with the availability of year-round fresh produce, as

15   well as more vegetarian dining options, it is easier than ever to adopt a plant-based lifestyle.

But for people who love to eat meat, it can be hard to make the switch to vegetarianism. For these people, fake meat products are a possible option.

20   And there has never been so many choices when it comes to fake meat. At supermarkets in many parts of the world, you can find an abundance of fake

burgers, sausages and nuggets that all taste like meat. People who miss the texture of meat but not the calories can find products that taste just like their favorite meat dishes. According to Sam Pearson, a chef and vegan restaurant owner, "Plant-based has undergone a dramatic shift over the years. Gone are the days when consumers expect vegan food to be tasteless vegetable mush."   25

And while there is evidence that vegetarianism reduces the risk of diseases such as diabetes, cancer and hypertension, the switch to fake meat might not be so healthy. Even though fake meat contains protein from things like mung beans, peas or soybeans, it often doesn't contain the same number   30 of vitamins and minerals as meat. Also, some fake meat products contain more saturated fats than real meat, as well as high amounts of sodium. A recent study has even shown that the carcinogen acrylamide is found in some plant-based meat products. According to TV chef Rachel Khoo, fake meat is "just another highly processed food with better marketing." Unscrupulous   35 companies sometimes advertise these products as heathier than meat when, in fact, they might not be.

This is not to say that all fake meat products are bad or that they shouldn't be consumed at all. Some quite healthy fake meat products have been made from *shiitake* mushrooms, for example. But if someone wants to   40 maintain a healthy vegetarian diet it is probably better to consume whole foods and stay away from processed foods as much as possible. Consumers should read the labels on what they buy carefully and not just assume that because something is meat-free that it is healthy. And for those vegetarians who really miss the taste of meat, keeping fake meat products as an occasional   45 treat might be the way to go.

COMPREHENSION

次の文を読み、本文の内容と合っていればT、そうでない場合はF を選択しましょう。

1. Lacto-ovo vegetarians only eat plant-based foods and dairy products. [T / F]
2. Eating fake meat isn't always healthy because there is no evidence that
   it reduces the risk of diseases such as diabetes, cancer and hypertension.

[T / F]

3. It might be a better to stay healthy by eating whole foods instead of processed foods as much as we can. [T / F]

4. We must not assume something is healthier just because it doesn't have meat. [T / F]

MAKE A SUMMARY 🎧 DL 78 💿 CD2-34

内容に合うように下線部に適切な語句や文を入れ、要約を完成させましょう。

More and more people are becoming vegetarians these days. The reasons for this are many. Some people want to ¹_____
_____. Others do it for their religion or to save money. There are ²_____. Some may eat eggs and dairy products while others eat only ³_____
_____. For those who like meat, becoming vegetarian may be difficult but ⁴_____. Yet meat-free food is not necessarily healthy so we have to be careful to read the labels on the food we buy. But fake meat might be an occasional treat for ⁵_____
_____.

HAVE YOUR SAY

以下は "If you decided to become a vegetarian, what are the reasons?" という問いに対するある学生の回答です。ペアを組み、これを自分たちに置き換えて、下線部を書き換えてみましょう（その後、クラスで発表してみましょう）。

I want to become a vegetarian because I have gained weight lately due to staying home for a long time. And I think it is costly and unhealthy to buy foods at convenience stores every day. The third reason is that I've learned consuming meat products has a negative effect on the environment. These reasons are why I've decided to become a vegetarian. At first, I'll try to eat Japanese food such as tofu and okara, which are made from soybeans. And someday I want to try fake meat products.

Unit

12 Cashless Society

キャッシュレス時代のビジネス

LISTENING

TARGET!

話者が 2 人以上の会話を聞き分け、理解しましょう   🎧 DL 79 💿 CD2-35

複数の話者がいる会話の聞き取りは、混同せずに各話者を頭の中で区別して聞きます。

1. 話者の間柄で区別する

・家族や友人同士の親しい間柄→とてもフランクな挨拶など

Hey, what's up? / What's new? / How's it going? / Hi there! / Hi ya!

・上司と部下、教師と学生など師弟関係→かしこまった表現など

May I ask? / Would you like some coffee?

・店員と客→決まった表現

May I take your order? / What can I get for you? / May I help you?

2. 主張の違いで区別する

・賛成 or 反対

（賛成する）I agree. / I'm for it. / I think you're right. / Absolutely.

（反対する）I don't really agree. / I have a different opinion. / I'm not sure about
that. / I don't think so.

・好き or 嫌い

（～が好き）like / prefer / be fond of / be a big fan of / be crazy about / be into

（～が嫌い）don't (doesn't) like ~ / dislike / hate

WARM UP   🎧 DL 80 💿 CD2-36

1 ～ 5 の音声を聞き、2 人の間柄を A ～ E から選びましょう。

1. (   ) **2.** (   ) **3.** (   ) **4.** (   ) **5.** (   )

A. 店の販売員と客   B. レストランの店員と客   C. 教師と学生
D. 親しい友人同士   E. 会社の上司と部下

TRY LISTENING   🎧 DL 81 💿 CD2-37

Alex、Chris、Ellie、Wendy が「レジ袋有料化」について話をしています。これを
聞き、「レジ袋有料化」について誰が賛成で反対かを書いてみましょう。

賛成者 [   ]   反対者 [   ]

CONVERSATION

DL 82 · CD2-38

A. 次の会話を聞き、（　　）に適切な語を入れましょう。会話のあとに問題が流れるので、適切な答えを a、b から選びましょう。

Beth and Erina have just eaten dinner at a restaurant.

Waiter: And how was your meal today?

Beth: It was wonderful, thanks. Can we get the check, please?

Waiter: Certainly. One moment, please.

Erina: Let me get it this time. You paid last time.

Beth: Are you sure? [1]_____?
We had a lot and the bill will probably be pretty high.

Erina: No, I insist. Besides, I just started using the new app FriendlyPay on my phone. [2]_____.

Beth: What's FriendlyPay?

Erina: It's an app that's connected to my bank account and allows me to pay for things through my phone. Most stores and restaurants are set up to accept the app now, so it's really convenient.

Beth: Cool. Well, you can still pay using FriendlyPay and
[3]_____.

Erina: No, really, it's OK.

Waiter: OK, here's your bill. Let me know [4]_____ _____.

Erina: That will be all thanks. Do you accept payment by FriendlyPay?

Waiter: [5]_____.

Erina: Oh, no!

Q1. **a.** Because the bill is very high and she doesn't want Beth to pay for it.
b. Because Erina wants to pay by using FriendlyPay.

Q2. **a.** They pay the bill by cash.　　**b.** Erina pays the bill by FriendlyPay.

B. クラスメートとペアを組み、完成した会話を発話練習してみましょう。

C. ＿＿＿部を参考に、同じペアで次の①または②のアプリを説明してみましょう。

① アプリ名（GoAnywhere）
　性能（銀行口座につながっていて、そのエリア内の交通料金を支払うことができる
② アプリ名（DoRemote）
　性能（家のデスクトップにつながっていて、外出中に家電の操作を行うことができる）

SHORT ANNOUNCEMENT　　DL 83　CD2-39

A. 次の録音メッセージの抜粋を聞き、下線部に適切な語句を入れましょう。

Hello, Beth. This is Adriana Jacobs ¹_____

_____. We are delighted that you have decided to use our service.
To answer your questions, yes, you can connect a credit card to the app.
You have the choice of having funds go directly from your bank account
or charged to your card. To set this up, just go to our homepage and click
on settings. There ²_____.
Secondly, regarding the refund on purchases, you will ³_____

_____ up to a total of ¥100,000. Please
give us a call again if you have any more questions. On behalf of our team
at FriendlyPay, I want to thank you for choosing us to help make your
cashless purchases as smooth as possible.

B. 次の文がメッセージの内容に合致している場合はT、そうでない場合はFを選択
しましょう。

1. The speaker called Beth but she didn't answer the call.　[T / F]

2. To set up the application of FriendlyPay, you need to call the bank first.
　[T / F]

3. On FriendlyPay, it is possible to get up to 150,000 yen back on your
purchases.　[T / F]

C. ペアを組み、　部を参考に次のような女性の特徴をアナウンスしてみましょう。
必要に応じて自分たちで情報を付け加えて話しましょう。

> ・一括で払うか分割で払うかのチョイスがあります。
> ・グループのすべてのメンバーを代表して、このボランティア活動に参加してくれた
> 　ことをお礼申し上げます。

81

READING

分詞構文の用法を理解し使いこなしましょう

1. 分詞の基本＝形容詞と同じ働きをします

[現在分詞] Look at those **dancing** people in the middle of the park.

[過去分詞] Mr. and Mrs. Cooper are both **retired** English teachers that worked at
our school.

2. 分詞構文＝接続詞の役割をして、時・理由・付帯状況・条件・譲歩などを表します

Running along the river (= When I was running...), I ran into a friend of mine.

Living in the countryside (= Since we live...), our house is very spacious.

3. 慣用的によく使われる分詞構文

judging from ~「～から判断すると」/ frankly speaking「率直にいうと」

generally speaking「一般的にいうと」/ speaking(Talking) of ~「～といえば」

providing (that) ~「仮に～として」/ regarding ~「～については」/ considering ~「～
を考慮すると」

GRAMMAR EXERCISE 1

日本文に合うように [　　　] 内の語句を並べ替え、分詞を加えて文を完成させましょう。

1. リチャードが新しい企画についてとても興奮する話を教えてくれた。

[has / a / told / just / Richard / story / very / me] about his new project.

_____

2. ほかの新聞に比べて、この新聞は安価で、内容も充実している。

[newspaper / cheap / other / a lot / newspapers / this / is / with / and / has / of / content].

_____

3. 正直にいうと、揚げた魚はあまり好きではないのです。

[really / I / honestly / like / don't / fish].

_____

GRAMMAR EXERCISE 2

日本語の意味になるように分詞を使って文を作ってみましょう。

1. 右に曲がって一区画歩くと、左側に博物館がありますよ。

_____

2. 仮に会議が行われなかったとしても、決定は変わることはありません。

_____

DEFINITION FOR READING

1 〜 5 の語句の定義として正しいものを a 〜 e から選んでみましょう。

1. predominantly (*l.*4) _____

2. transaction (*l.*7) _____

3. ubiquitous (*l.*20) _____

4. incentive (*l.*30) _____

5. hygienic (*l.*43) _____

a. appearing or found everywhere

b. clean and free of bacteria

c. mostly or mainly

d. something that encourages you to work harder

e. a business deal such as buying and selling something

READING

🎧 DL 84   ⊙ CD2-40 ～ ⊙ CD2-44

次の文章を読み、あとに続く問題に答えましょう。

Is Japan Becoming a Cashless Society?

Opening a wallet full of cash and fumbling for coins in front of a cashier is a common occurrence in Japan. Similarly, using point cards and coupons to make the price cheaper when paying by cash happens all the time. Japan has predominantly been a cash-based society. Things are changing, however. Digital forms of payment are becoming more prevalent, such as credit cards, mobile wallets, and prepaid cards like Suica and Pasmo. In fact, the Japanese government is seeking to raise the amount of cashless transactions to 40% by 2027, nearly double what it is now at about 20%.

Raising the number of digital transactions will have multiple benefits to society. First, with Japan's declining population and labor shortage, moving to cashless systems will put less strain on the work force. It is currently estimated that the handling of cash costs nearly ¥1 trillion annually in Japan. Furthermore, shifting from cash to digital transactions will allow the government to more easily track the flow of money and make tax collecting more efficient and accurate.

Considering the benefits of a cashless lifestyle, it is a puzzling fact that Japan has been slow to move away from using physical currency compared to other countries. There are several reasons for this. First, Japan has a low crime rate and people feel comfortable carrying money without the fear of theft. ATMs are also ubiquitous so it's easy to get cash whenever necessary. Also, some people are concerned about privacy and feel that digital purchases

5

10

15

20

might allow companies to collect information about their purchase histories, which could then be used for other purposes. Another reason that many Japanese still use cash is that many stores and restaurants only accept cash. For example, as of 2020, looking at the restaurant review website Tabelog shows that less than 60% of restaurants in Tokyo accept credit cards. With such practices in place, it is discouraging for people to move to cashless payments.

Recognizing this situation, some major companies are providing incentives for people to go cashless. Line Corp., the popular messaging app company, has been promoting their Line Pay service, which allows people to pay in stores via QR codes, prepaid cards or smartphones. To encourage businesses to use the system, they have been providing the scanning devices to stores for free for the first six months of use. PayPay Corp., a mobile payment firm run by SoftBank Group Corp. and Yahoo Japan, has developed an app that allows customers to pay digitally. To motivate people to use the app, PayPay started a campaign where customers who made purchases using the app could get a 20% rebate on their purchases for up to ¥50,000 per month.

Recent world events such as the COVID-19 pandemic have also made cashless payments more desirable, as they are more hygienic. This, along with the combination of government encouragement and incentives from private industry, seems to be causing a shift in the way many Japanese consumers make their purchases. The trend will, no doubt, continue into the foreseeable future.

COMPREHENSION

次の文を読み、本文の内容と合っていれば T、そうでない場合は F を選択しましょう。

1. By 2027, the Japanese government is trying to raise the amount of cashless transactions to 20%.　　　　　　　　　　　　　　　　　　[T / F]

2. In Japan, handing of cash costs almost ¥1 trillion a year now.　　[T / F]

3. More than 40% of restaurants in Tokyo don't accept credit cards at the Tabelog website. [T / F]

4. To broaden their business, Line Corp. provides free scanners to stores for three months. [T / F]

MAKE A SUMMARY 🎧 DL 85 💿 CD2-45

内容に合うように下線部に適切な語句や文を入れ、要約を完成させましょう。

Japan has been a cash-based society, however, digital forms of payment are ¹_____. By using digital transactions, we don't have to worry about labor shortage and also the government ²_____ more easily. Even so, Japan has been slow to ³_____, because Japan has ⁴_____ and people feel comfortable carrying cash. People are also concerned about having their digital purchases tracked. Moreover, many stores still accept only cash. Some major companies have been promoting for people to go cashless, for example, ⁵_____ on their purchases. The cashless trend will continue into the future.

HAVE YOUR SAY

以下は "Is a cashless society really beneficial for us?" という問いに対するある学生の回答です。ペアを組み、これを自分たちに置き換えて、下線部を書き換えてみましょう（その後、クラスで発表してみましょう）。

There are both good points and bad points for a cashless society. Some of the merits are that we don't need to carry around a heavy wallet, so we can go out with minimum items. Moreover, by using a cashless system we can get some points to use for future shopping. However, there are also some weak points. I tend to spend too much as I don't feel like I'm spending real money. I have to be very careful with that. Hopefully these systems will improve in the future.

13 New Energy Source

再生可能な新しいエネルギー

ISTENING

TARGET!

会話の場面を特定して、内容理解をスムーズに 🎧 DL 86 💿 CD2-46

特定の場所で使われる表現や語句に着目します。

1. レストランなどの店内
（店員）May I help you? / How would you like your steak prepared?
（客）May I ask you something? / Could I have the menu, please?

2. 交通関連
（駅や空港など）Would you prefer a window seat or an aisle seat? / Do you have something to declare? / The flight has been delayed due to bad weather.
（乗り物内）This train is bound for Shinjuku. / Please check that your seatbelt is securely fastened.

3. 電話
Could you connect me with Mr. Brown? / May I speak to Ken? / Please hold the line. / I am afraid Mr. Brown is on another line. / Ms. Scott is not available right now. / Would you like to leave a message?

WARM UP 🎧 DL 87 💿 CD2-47

1～5の音声を聞き、これを聞いている側がどの場所にいるかをA、Bから選びましょう。

1. **A.** カフェの座席　　　**B.** カフェの注文カウンター　　　　（　　　　）
2. **A.** 飛行機の機内　　　**B.** 空港の搭乗ゲート　　　　　　　（　　　　）
3. **A.** 駅の券売機前　　　**B.** 駅のホーム　　　　　　　　　　（　　　　）
4. **A.** オフィスの座席　　**B.** 電話ボックス　　　　　　　　　（　　　　）
5. **A.** ホテルの室内　　　**B.** ホテルのチェックインカウンター　（　　　　）

TRY LISTENING 🎧 DL 88 💿 CD2-48

次の1、2の会話を聞き、どこで、誰と誰が話しているかを記入してみましょう。

1. どこで　_____
   誰が　　（　　　　　　　　　）と（　　　　　　　　　　）

2. どこで　_____
   誰が　　（　　　　　　　　　）と（　　　　　　　　　　）

CONVERSATION

DL 89   CD2-49

A. 次の会話を聞き、（　　）に適切な語を入れましょう。会話のあとに問題が流れるので、適切な答えを a ～ c から選びましょう。

Three students are chatting about their class.

Paul: Today's class was really interesting, don't you think?

Beth: Yes, but it was a little hard to understand for me. I got confused when the teacher was talking about [1]_____ _____.

Paul: You mean the anode and cathode?

Beth: Yes, that part. And I always have to remind myself that electrons move [2]_____ _____.

Brandon: I thought that part about [3]_____ was cool!

Paul: Yes, that was pretty amazing, wasn't it?

Beth: By the way, Paul, that looks so good. What is it?

Paul: It's lasagna. It's today's special.

Beth: Ah, nice. [4]_____.

Brandon: [5]_____. Shall we go together?

Beth: Sure. I wonder what is on the menu today. Hopefully something Italian!

Brandon: Shall we go now?

Beth: OK. And when we get back, will both of you please help me review electrodes?!

Q1. **a.** classroom **b.** cafeteria **c.** library

Q2. **a.** Paul and Brandon **b.** Beth and Brandon **c.** Paul and Beth

B. クラスメートとペアを組み、完成した会話を発話練習してみましょう。

C. ＿＿＿部を参考に、同じペアで次の①または②のシチュエーションで会話をしてみましょう。

① 映画に一緒に行こうと誘う→（答え）「もちろん。劇場ではどんな映画が上映中なんだろう」

② ピクニックに一緒に行こうと誘う→（答え）「もちろん。午後の天気はどんな感じなんだろう」

SHORT ANNOUNCEMENT

A. 次の授業音声の一部を聞き、下線部に適切な語句を入れましょう。

Good afternoon everyone. Today we will be talking about electrodes. An electrode is a type of electrical conductor that makes contact with non-metallic surfaces within a circuit and ¹_____ _____. Some examples of non-metallic surfaces are semiconductors, electrolytes, or air. In fact, recently electrodes have even been connected to bacteria that ²_____ _____ in the air. It is quite amazing, really. The common type of electrode that everyone is familiar with is the kind found on a battery, usually marked positive and negative. The electrode at the positive end is called a cathode and the electrode at the negative end is called an anode. Electrons enter the battery from the cathode and leave from the anode. But remember, electrical current flows opposite the movement of electrons, so ³_____. Are there any questions so far?

B. 次の文がメッセージの内容に合致している場合は T、そうでない場合は F を選択しましょう。

1. An electrode is an electrical conductor that carries electric current into non-metallic surfaces.　　　　　　　　　　　　　　　　[T / F]

2. Bacteria connected to electrodes can generate electricity from moisture in the air.　　　　　　　　　　　　　　　　　　　　　[T / F]

3. The electrical current moves from the cathode to the anode.　[T / F]

C. ペアを組み、　　部を参考に次のような留学プログラムについて説明してみましょう。必要に応じて自分たちで情報を付け加えて話しましょう。

> ・海外留学生プログラム（overseas student programs）にはホームステイ、語学学校研修、国際キャンプなどがあります。
> ・最も一般的なものは大学のもので、たいていは大学の留学生事務局で提供しています。

88

EADING

いろいろな比較表現で程度をより細かく説明してみましょう

1. 比較の基本

（原級）This pasta wasn't **as (so) bad as** I thought it would be.

（比較級）It's getting **harder** and **harder** to get a job in this country.

（最上級）This is **the most impressive** novel I've ever read.

2. 比較を用いた表現

The older you get, **the weaker** your memory becomes.

（年をとるほど記憶力は弱くなる）

He got **more** red cards **than any other** player on the team. ＝最上級の意味になる

（彼はチームでほかの誰よりも多くのレッドカードを受けた）

Sitting next to her boyfriend, she seemed **as relaxed as can be**.

（ボーイフレンドの隣に座って、彼女はこの上なくリラックスしているようだった）

ほかに no more than / no less than / nothing less than / might (may) as well など

GRAMMAR EXERCISE 1

日本文に合うように（　　）に適語を入れ、文を完成させましょう。

1. あなたは彼女の息子であることを誇りに思ってよい。

You might (　　　　　) (　　　　　) (　　　　　) (　　　　　) of being her son.

2. 彼の突然の辞退は裏切りも同然だ。

His sudden withdrawal is (　　　　　) (　　　　　) (　　　　　) a betrayal.

3. 最新のスマホは一つ前のモデルのおよそ 1.5 倍の価格である。

The latest smartphones costs nearly 1.5 (　　　　　) (　　　　　) (　　　　　)

(　　　　　) the previous model.

4. 増築後、そこは地域で三番目に大きなホテルとなった。

After the extension, it became (　　　　　) (　　　　　) (　　　　　) hotel in

the area.

GRAMMAR EXERCISE 2

日本語の意味になるように文を作ってみましょう。

1. 本をたくさん読めば読むほど、あなたの生活はより素晴らしくなる。

_____

2. 彼はほかのどの候補者よりもその仕事に適任だった。

_____

DEFINITION FOR READING

1〜5の語句の定義として正しいものをa〜eから選んでみましょう。

1. imperative (*l.*2) _____

2. sediment (*l.*9) _____

3. harness (*l.*6) _____

4. groundbreaking (*l.*15) _____

5. gradient (*l.*38) _____

a. making new discoveries; using a new method

b. the degree to which the ground slopes

c. very important and needing immediate attention or action

d. the solid material that settles at the bottom of liquid

e. control and make use of natural resources, especially to produce energy

READING

DL 91　CD2-51 〜 CD2-55

次の文章を読み、あとに続く問題に答えましょう。

Electric Bacteria: A New Source of Energy?

　　With global resources diminishing, the race to find alternative energy sources is more imperative than ever. Solar power, wind energy, and hydroelectricity are just some of the technologies that have been developed to supply our future energy needs. But one team from the University of
5　Massachusetts (UMass) has discovered a way of generating electricity literally out of thin air. They are able to do this by harnessing the power of bacteria.

　　The bacteria that allows the generation of electricity is called Geobacter. These bacteria make protein nanowires which are used to transfer electrons to other bacteria or sediment in the surrounding environment. When
10　the electrons are transferred, a small electrical current is created. Some years ago, scientists experimented with Geobacter and discovered that the bacteria can be used to transfer electrons from organic material to metallic material. Since then, efforts have been made to harness the power of Geobacter to make energy.
15　Recently, a groundbreaking discovery made Geobacter even more promising when Liu Xiaomeng, a graduate student at UMass, observed that, on occasion, Geobacter nanowires spontaneously produced electrical current.

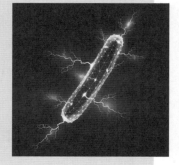

　　Working with Yao Jun, his adviser, Xiaomeng created a device by
20　making a film of bacterial nanowires and putting it between two gold plates, which functioned as electrodes. The top plate was smaller than the bottom

plate so some of the nanowire film was directly exposed to the air. They left the device alone and found that it generated electricity for around 20 hours. The device also worked when plates made of carbon were used. But, because carbon is not a good source for electrons, the nanowires could not be drawing   25
the electrons from the plates. The researchers further observed that the device would work in the light or dark, so the electric current was not caused by chemical reactions triggered by light. So where was the electric current coming from? It seemed that the nanowires were generating electricity from the air!   30

Xiaomeng and Jun got an important clue when they put the device in a chamber with low humidity and the current decreased. So, moisture was an important factor in the process. By exposing the nanowires to various levels of humidity, the scientists discovered that air with about 45% humidity is best for generating current. However, the nanowires were able to function with   35
various levels of moisture in the air. The way the process seems to work is that when just the top of the nanowire film is exposed to air, it absorbs water, and this creates a moisture gradient. When the absorbed water separates into hydrogen and oxygen ions, a charge builds up and an electric current begins to flow from the top to the bottom of the film.   40

The implications of this discovery are huge. Being able to get renewable energy from moisture in the air could make electricity production much cheaper and less wasteful than it is now. There are still many factors to consider, however. The exact way the nanowires work is still unknown, and more research needs to be done. But Geobacter and its nanowires have not   45
only generated electricity, they have generated hope.

COMPREHENSION

次の文を読み、本文の内容と合っていれば T、そうでない場合は F を選択しましょう。

1. Xiaomeng found Geobacter can generate electrical current automatically.

[T / F]

2. Geobacter can produce electrical current by a chemical reaction triggered by light.

[T / F]

3. The plates made of carbon were not suitable for Geobacter to generate
electricity. [T / F]

4. Humidity is an important factor for Geobacter to produce electrical current.
[T / F]

MAKE A SUMMARY

🎧 DL 92　◉ CD2-56

内容に合うように下線部に適切な語句や文を入れ、要約を完成させましょう。

One research team at the University of Massachusetts found that
¹_____. These
bacteria, Geobacter, make protein nanowires which are used to transfer
electrons to other bacteria or sediment in their environment. When the
electrons are transferred, ²_____.
The researchers further observed that electric current was not caused
by ³_____. Another finding
shows that ⁴_____ is best for
generating current. Being able to get renewable energy from moisture
in the air could make electricity production ⁵_____
_____ it is now.

HAVE YOUR SAY

以下は "What is one major innovation or discovery in our lifetime?" という問
いに対するある学生の回答です。ペアを組み、これを自分たちに置き換えて、下線部
を書き換えてみましょう（その後、クラスで発表してみましょう）。

> I think the most remarkable innovation in our lifetime is the
> internet. With the internet, we can talk with people wherever they
> live whenever we want. Furthermore, we can buy whatever we
> want online easily. Recently, it is common that we study or work
> remotely from our school or office by making use of video meeting
> applications. That is how the internet has made a huge impact
> on our lives. So I believe that the internet will cause even more
> positive changes in the future!

14 Future of Drones

ドローンで変わる未来の生活

ISTENING

> **TARGET!**
>
> ### キーワードから話題を推測し、内容を把握しましょう 🎧 DL 93 ◉ CD2-57
>
> キーワードから主題をキャッチすることで、リスニングの理解度はグッと高まります。
>
> **1. 冒頭に述べられる主題をキャッチする**
> Today, we are pleased to announce the launch of **our new streaming service**.（スピーチの冒頭）
>
> **2. 複数回登場する語に着目する（品詞が変わることも）**
> FOB Corporation has announced the release of its new system using their unique **AI** technology. This **AI** technology, which is called FOB-**AI**, reproduces ... ,
>
> **3. いくつかのキーワードから話題を推測する**
> face... gate... ID →顔認証システムの話　　race... hate... protest →人種差別の話

WARM UP　　🎧 DL 94 ◉ CD2-58

次の１〜３の文を聞き、（　　）に適語を補って文を完成させましょう。完成したら、それが何の話題かを書いてみましょう。

1. When you take a (　　　　　) of something nearby in the dark, put your

(　　　　　) in macro mode and turn the (　　　　　) to forced (　　　　)

mode.　　　　　　　　　　　　　　　　話題 [　　　　　　　　　　　]

2. Today I will introduce you to some tips for finding a nice (　　　　　) to

(　　　　) in (　　　　　). Before that, you need to know the (　　　　)

(　　　　) in (　　　　) are now definitely the highest in (　　　　)

(　　　　).　　　　　　　　　　　　　　話題 [　　　　　　　　　　　]

3. It is a type of (　　　　) (　　　　　) which is used among the members

of a (　　　　) community and is not issued by a central (　　　　　).

話題 [　　　　　　　　　　　]

TRY LISTENING　　🎧 DL 95 ◉ CD2-59

次の１〜４の音声を聞き、何についての話かを日本語で書いてみましょう。

1. (　　　　　　　　　　)　　**2.** (　　　　　　　　　　)

3. (　　　　　　　　　　)　　**4.** (　　　　　　　　　　)

CONVERSATION

A. 次の会話を聞き、（　　）に適切な語を入れましょう。会話のあとに問題が流れるので、適切な答えを a、b から選びましょう。

Beth is talking to Paul and Brandon while they are making something.

Beth: Hey, what are you guys doing? [1]_____?

Paul: It sure is. [2]_____.
My parents gave it to me for my birthday.

Beth: Cool! You're so lucky! I've always wanted to operate one. Can I help?

Paul: Sure, though we're just about done. We've already attached the propellers and motors, now we just need to [3]_____
_____.

Brandon: I think the camera goes on that mount right there. It doesn't need any screws. It just snaps on.

Paul: There, done! Let's go try it out! I just need to [4]_____
_____. It shouldn't be that hard.

Brandon: [5]_____, though.
Are we allowed to fly it in the neighborhood?

Paul: No, city regulations don't permit it. Why don't we head to the park? It's legal there.

Beth: Yes, I've seen people flying them there before.

Q1. **a.** They were quarreling with how to create a drone and Beth helped them make up.

　　　b. They were putting together the parts of a drone.

Q2. **a.** Flying their drone may disturb the neighbors.
　　　b. Flying their drone is hard so they need to study before flying.

B. クラスメートとペアを組み、完成した会話を発話練習してみましょう。

C. ▒▒▒部を参考に、同じペアで次の①または②のシチュエーションで会話をしてみましょう。

① この美術館で写真を撮ることができるかを聞く→（答え）美術館のルールで許されていない。

② そのテーマパークに食料を持ち込んでもよいかを聞く→（答え）テーマパークのルールで持ち込みは許可されている。

SHORT ANNOUNCEMENT

DL 97 CD2-61

A. 次の宣伝メッセージの抜粋を聞き、下線部に適切な語句を入れましょう。

If you are new to the world of unmanned aircraft systems and want to learn more about this exciting new technology, come to the Alta Drone Park. The park is provided as a resource to encourage ¹ _____. We feature a soccer-field-sized facility with private airspace that gives members of the community a place to learn how to fly drones ² _____. We also have instructors on site to help you ³ _____. For those seeking to go further and obtain certification, we offer a full training program that will get you ready to operate drones in a variety of commercial and governmental positions. Anyone seeking to operate a drone at the park may do so by first scheduling their flight with the park office. First-time flyers will be required to complete a brief session on the safe and appropriate use of the facility.

B. 次の文がメッセージの内容に合致している場合は T、そうでない場合は F を選択しましょう。

1. The purpose of the park is to utilize drone technology for soccer fields.

[T / F]

2. There are several limitations you need to know in order to fly drones in this park.

[T / F]

3. Even if you fly drones for the first time, you don't need to learn how to fly it in the park.

[T / F]

C. ペアを組み、　　部を参考に次のようなトレーニングジムの特徴をアナウンスしてみましょう。必要に応じて自分たちで情報を付け加えて話しましょう。

- よりハードな肉体改造（body-making）トレーニングをお求めの人たちのために、我々はあなたを極限まで（to the extreme）鍛える画期的なプログラムを提供します。
- 初回の入会者（members）は ID カードの提出と登録が必要になります。

 **R**EADING

関係詞の種類・機能を理解し、使いこなしましょう

1. **関係代名詞**＝主格、所有格、目的格があり、目的格はしばしば省略される
   The man I met on the street works at a bank. →目的格の省略（the man whom I met）
   She lent me some DVDs, **which** were less interesting than I expected.
      →非制限用法（コンマ＋関係詞）。DVD のすべてが less interesting ではない。
   関係代名詞 what　I didn't understand what they said. →先行詞を含む（the thing）
2. **関係副詞**＝関係詞節中で副詞の役割を果たす。where, when, why, how など
   She went to New York, **where** she studied economics and politics.
      →先行詞が固有名詞の場合も非制限用法
3. **複合関係代名詞**＝ whenever, wherever, whichever, whoever, whatever, however
   Whoever is responsible for this problem will be fired.「だれでも」

GRAMMAR EXERCISE 1

日本文に合うように（　　）に適語を入れ、文を完成させましょう。

1. ジャクソンさんはこのようにして有名なドレスデザイナーになった。

   （　　　　　）（　　　　　）（　　　　　　）Ms. Jackson became a world famous

   dress designer.

2. 私たちがすべきことは、いつ災害が起きても平常心でいることだ。

   （　　　　　　　）（　　　　　　　） have to do is to keep calm （　　　　　　　） a

   disaster happens.

3. 彼女はゲイナーさんから書類を受け取ったが、どこかで紛失してしまった。

   She received a document from Mr. Gainer, （　　　　　）（　　　　）（　　　　　）

   （　　　　） somewhere.

GRAMMAR EXERCISE 2

日本語の意味になるように関係詞を使って文を作ってみましょう。

1. 私にとって難しいことは、朝のラッシュアワーに車を運転することだ。

   _____

2. その理論についてどんなに説明したところで、彼らには理解できない。

   _____

DEFINITION FOR READING

1 〜 5 の語句の定義として正しいものを a 〜 e から選んでみましょう。

1. unmanned (*l.*2) _____
2. fertilizer (*l.*8) _____
3. tether (*l.*15) _____
4. thriving (*l.*43) _____
5. surveillance (*l.*45) _____

a. the act of carefully watching a person
b. a type of nutrition for plants to grow better
c. growing or developing well
d. without any operator
e. use (a smartphone) in order to connect devices to the internet

READING

DL 98   CD2-62 ～ CD2-67

次の文章を読み、あとに続く問題に答えましょう。

How Drone Technology Is Changing Our Way of Life

One of the hot topics of modern technology is the use of drones. Originally developed for warfare, these remotely controlled, unmanned aircraft are experiencing an increasing amount of applications not connected to the military.

One such use of drones is in precision agriculture, which is a type of farming management where people use drones to monitor crops. The drones observe and record data that is used to improve productivity. For example, the data might show which crops need water or where soil might need fertilizer. As another example, some vineyards are using drones to help them make wine. Sometimes grapes become diseased and that disease can quickly spread to other grapes, causing serious damage. Drones can identify and flag diseased grapes quickly, enabling crops to be saved. What would normally take a week for workers walking up and down rows of vines takes only minutes for drones to do with nearly 95% accuracy.

Another application for drones is tethering mobile data signals. When Hurricane Maria hit Puerto Rico in 2017, it severely damaged the island's electrical grid and communication systems. As a result, mobile phone connections were lost, and many people were left without a way to contact their loved ones. To quickly fix the situation, the American phone company AT&T sent in a drone that beamed mobile data signals for 65 kilometers in all directions. Art Pregler is the person who oversaw the project. Regarding the

5

10

15

20

drone, he said, "As soon as we turned it on, people just started connecting to it instantly." Facebook has also experimented with the use of drones to provide internet access to remote areas in the world.

25   Drones are also revolutionizing how packages are delivered. Amazon is working on a delivery system called Prime Air, which will use drones to deliver light weight packages in less than 30 minutes. This technology could

30 also be used in the future for time-sensitive health emergencies, such as medicine or organ shipments. Some drones are equipped with defibrillators which are devices that restore a normal heartbeat by delivering an electric shock to the heart. These drones also have a camera and laptop with a speaker equipped so someone could be guided through how

35 to use it. Sending one of these drones ahead of an ambulance could save precious time in the case of a medical emergency.

        An industry whose use of drones is very well known is the film industry. Movies and TV shows often feature scenes where the camera is moving over the tops of buildings or other public places. The use of drones

40 has provided videographers and photographers with new opportunities to express their creativity. Hobbyists, as well, have embraced this technology and the use of drones for private use is thriving.

        With this new technology comes many problems, as well. With drones' capacity for surveillance, there are concerns for privacy. There are

45 also concerns about how safe unmanned vehicles are and the possibility of accidents. There are certainly many factors to be considered as drones become more prevalent in our daily lives.

COMPREHENSION
次の文を読み、本文の内容と合っていれば T、そうでない場合は F を選択しましょう。

1. Drones harvest crops and put them in bags in place of workers.   [T / F]

2. When a huge hurricane occurred, drones found sufferers and flagged them quickly.   [T / F]

3. Drones carry people who require emergency medical care to the hospital.

[T / F]

4. Drones enables videographers to shoot scenes taken from overhead.   [T / F]

MAKE A SUMMARY

 DL 99   CD2-68

内容に合うように下線部に適切な語句や文を入れ、要約を完成させましょう。

 Remotely controlled drones are becoming the focus of increased attention. People seek various applications of using drones. One example is in precision agriculture. Drones observe and record data that shows [1]_____
_____. Another example is tethering mobile data signals. When a strong hurricane hit Puerto Rico and [2]_____, drones connected mobile signals in place of damaged communication systems. The third example is delivering. Drones changed [3]_____
_____. In the future, they could also be used for [4]_____
_____like delivering defibrillators. Drones are also used in the film industry to feature scenes from tops of buildings and so on. But there are also concerns about [5]_____
and the possibility of accidents.

HAVE YOUR SAY

以下は "If you have a drone, what would you like to do?" という問いに対するある学生の回答です。ペアを組み、下線部を自分たちに置き換えて、配布された記入用紙に書いてみましょう（その後、クラスで発表してみましょう）。

> If I have a drone, I would like to shoot a video of the lake in my hometown. Then, I will watch the video with my grandparents because they are too old to go out to the lake. In order to do so, I have to learn how to handle a drone and shoot a video with it. Other than shooting the video, I'd like to participate in drone racing with my friends and deliver some nice souvenirs to my grandparents.

The Pandemic and the Environment

·······················

パンデミックと環境問題

ISTENING

TARGET!

会話の主題・要点を聞き取りましょう   🎧 DL 100 💿 CD2-69

英語のプレゼンやスピーチの構成は introduction / body / conclusion となっており、introduction で言いたい主張などを述べ、conclusion に introduction で話した内容をまとめるパターンが基本で、この最初と最後の要点を確実に聞き取ることが重要です。

1. Introduction で主題・要点を言う際の表現（これから何について話すか）
I'm talking about ... / This presentation is about ... / Today, I will be describing ~ / present a speech on ~ / Let me begin my presentation by ~

2. Conclusion で主題・要点を言う際の表現（これまでの話をまとめる）
Let me summarize ~ ... , / In summary / Today we have examined ... / As a result / Eventually / Finally / To wrap up, ...

WARM UP   🎧 DL 101 💿 CD2-70

次の 1 ～ 3 はスピーチやプレゼンの introduction 部分です。これらを聞き、これから話者が何について話すかを ［　　］ に記入してみましょう。

1. ［   ］ 2. ［   ］
3. ［   ］

TRY LISTENING   🎧 DL 102 💿 CD2-71

次は Warm Up 設問 3 のスピーチの conclusion 部分です。これを聞き、下線部に適語を補って文を完成させましょう。

Now, let me summarize this workshop. I think that you were able to learn three ways to cope with stress when you go abroad. One way is to _____
_____ , such as listening to music and reading books. Another way is to _____ . By finding a friend to communicate with, you can ease your stress. Finally, _____
_____ is also a useful way to familiarize yourself with your new location.

CONVERSATION

🎧 DL 103　◉ CD2-72

A. 次の会話を聞き、（　）に適切な語を入れましょう。会話のあとに問題が流れるので、適切な答えを a、b から選びましょう。

Three students are talking about their experiences during the pandemic.

Paul:　　Hey, what did you guys do when you were self-quarantined during the COVID-19 pandemic?

Brandon: I just ¹＿＿＿＿＿＿＿＿＿＿＿＿＿＿＿＿＿＿

＿＿＿＿＿＿＿＿＿＿＿＿＿＿＿.

Paul:　　Yeah, me, too.

Erina:　Not me. I used the time for studying. I took several online classes and ²＿＿＿＿＿＿＿

＿＿＿＿＿＿＿＿＿＿＿＿＿＿＿＿.

Paul:　　That's great. I should have done something like that.

Brandon: One thing interesting happened, though. My sister and I saw a fox walking on the street outside our house!

Paul:　　Really?! That's cool! Did you go out and try to get close to it?

Brandon: No. We just watched it from the window. We heard on the news that ³＿＿＿＿＿＿＿＿＿＿＿＿＿＿＿＿＿.

Paul:　　⁴＿＿＿＿＿＿＿＿＿＿＿＿＿＿＿＿＿＿＿＿＿ if I were you.

Erina:　I've heard of similar stories in other cities, too. Since all of us were inside self-quarantining, ⁵＿＿＿＿＿＿＿＿＿＿＿

＿＿＿＿＿＿＿＿＿＿＿.

Paul:　　The world has changed in so many ways since COVID-19, hasn't it?

Q1. **a.** Taking online classes and studying　　**b.** Surfing the Internet and watching TV

Q2. **a.** They didn't have to fear coming to the city while most people stayed inside.
b. They were so hungry that they needed to find something to eat in the city.

B. クラスメートとペアを組み、完成した会話を発話練習してみましょう。

C. ペアを組み、　　部の Paul の発言に対する返答を Brandon と Erina になったつもりで考えて、英語で表現してみましょう。

① Yes の場合は、具体的にどこが変わったか。
② No の場合は、具体的にどこが変わらなかったか。

SHORT ANNOUNCEMENT

A. 次のラジオ番組を聞き、下線部に適切な語句を入れましょう。

Good evening everyone. This is KWTV News at Eleven. ¹_____
_____ due to the COVID-19
pandemic. Tonight, we have an unusual and, perhaps, slightly amusing
story for you. Foxes have been spotted roaming the downtown areas.
Fox sightings are normally quite rare. We have not received a report of
a sighting for some months, even in the wild. But earlier today, several
were spotted at various places around the city. Animal safety experts say
that while most of us remain home in self-quarantine, ²_____
_____. While it may be
tempting to try and go out and get some photos of these cute critters,
experts advise us not to do so. While foxes are generally considered not to
be dangerous, ³_____.
So, if you see some roaming your neighborhood, stay home and stay safe.
And now for our next story of the evening…

B. 次の文がメッセージの内容に合致している場合は T、そうでない場合は F を選択
しましょう。

1. About 20 days have passed since the city went into lockdown.   [T / F]

2. Animal safety experts are confident that foxes are roaming the city.   [T / F]

3. You can easily take pictures of roaming foxes because they are generally
   considered tame.   [T / F]

C. ペアを組み、 　　部を参考に次のような健康関連のアドバイスをしてみましょう。
   必要に応じて自分たちで情報を付け加えて話しましょう。

> ・夜中に甘いものを食べたい誘惑に駆られるかもしれませんが、専門家はそうしない
>   よう助言しています。
> ・なので、肥満になりたくなければ、夜の 8 時前には夕食を食べ、10 時前には寝て
>   ください。

EADING

仮定法の基本と応用をマスターしましょう

1. 仮定法過去＝現在の事実とは異なる仮定

If I **were** an animal expert, I **would research** about the peculiar behavior of foxes during lockdown.

2. 仮定法過去完了＝過去の事実とは異なる仮定

If we **had been** more cautious, the accident **would have been** avoided.

3. If 節を用いない仮定法

Had I known, I would have taken pictures on my camera. → if の省略

Without your help, we would never save the environment. →「～がなければ…だろう」

Such a strange thing might never happen again. →名詞に仮定が含まれる「そんな奇妙なことは～だろう」

GRAMMAR EXERCISE 1

日本語に合うように（　　）に適語を入れ、文を完成させましょう。

1. もし私が料理が上手ならば、皆に美味しい料理を振る舞うだろうに。

（　　　　）（　　　　）（　　　　　　　） a good cook, （　　　　）（　　　　　　　） offer everyone delicious dishes.

2. もう少し知識を持っていたら、私たちはもっと楽しめたのに！

（　　　　） a little more knowledge, we （　　　　）（　　　　）（　　　　） more fun!

3. ワンさんの代わりに彼がカナダ支社に行ければいいのに。

（　　）（　　　　　） he （　　　　　　）（　　　　　） to the Canadian branch instead of Mr. Wang.

GRAMMAR EXERCISE 2

[　　] 内の語句を並べ替えて文を完成させましょう。

1. [scientist, / if / invent / I / a / I / tool / a / helpful / were / would] for disabled people. _____

2. [she / her / have / arrived / she / earlier, / met / had / could] favorite actor.

_____

3. Another [bankruptcy / yen / have / his / could / company / from / saved / 20 million]. _____

DEFINITION FOR READING

1〜5の語句の定義として正しいものをa〜eから選んでみましょう。

1. subside (*l*.4)　　　　＿＿＿　　**a.** fall or drop steeply

2. induce (*l*.21)　　　　＿＿＿　　**b.** a brief, partial view or sight

3. unprecedented (*l*.16)　＿＿＿　　**c.** bring about, cause things to happen

4. glimpse (*l*.19)　　　　＿＿＿　　**d.** never done or happened before

5. plummet (*l*.23)　　　　＿＿＿　　**e.** go down, become quiet, less active

READING

 DL 105 ～ CD2-74 ～ CD2-78

次の文章を読み、あとに続く問題に答えましょう。

The Bounceback of Nature in the Wake of COVID-19

　　The COVID-19 pandemic brought many difficulties both to human lives and economies. It also caused environmental changes that some see as beneficial. As people across the planet began to self-quarantine and daily activities subsided, the quality of the air improved. There were also changes
5　in regard to wildlife and biodiversity. Experts suggest that we learn from this time and use the information to improve our relationship with the environment.

　　While it is too early to say what the full impact of COVID-19 will be on the environment, carbon emissions have dropped significantly. In March 2020,
10　after a month of restricted activities, China experienced an 18% reduction in carbon emissions and across Europe, reductions were as much as 40 to 60%. In the UK, road traffic decreased by 70% and similar statistics were reported in the US where passenger vehicle traffic dropped by 40%. At the time, Rob Jackson, the chair of Global Carbon
15　Project, said "The drop in emissions is global and unprecedented." Drops in carbon emissions, along with improving air quality, reduce the risks of asthma, lung disease and heart attacks. Perhaps this is a glimpse of what the world
20　would look like if there were not any fossil fuels.

　　The fossil fuel industry was hit hard by the lockdowns induced

by COVID-19. With fewer drivers on the road and planes in the sky, fuel consumption plummeted and the price of oil went down to two-thirds of what it was in 2019. From an environmental perspective, this could be seen as a positive trend as oil is the biggest source of carbon emissions. Some analysts   25
suggest that this could be the beginning of the end for oil. If that be the case, new forms of energy will need to be developed.

Along with the changes in air quality, there were also shifts in wildlife populations because of the pandemic. As humans stayed indoors, animals came out more. For example, coyotes were seen on the Golden Gate bridge in   30
San Francisco. Wild boars were seen in Barcelona. In Wales, some cities saw peacocks, goats and sheep strutting through the streets. The decrease in traffic resulted in less roadkill by cars and trucks. Also, many local governments delayed cutting grass on roadsides, which resulted in more wildflowers and other flora that are a good source of pollen for bees. It might seem like nature   35
flourished in the wake of COVID-19, but some environmental campaigners say this is a misconception. While there was a temporary recovery of nature in wealthy, industrial nations, poorer countries feared that with less revenue, there would be less money to pay conservation personnel. This could result in increased illegal poaching, mining and logging.   40

Overall, though, there appears to have been some benefits to the environment because of the decrease in human activity during lockdown. As we return to our normal lives, it is important that we learn from this experience. Government leaders, scientists and activists are calling for a public debate so that our recovery from COVID-19 can bring focus to creating   45
more clean energy technology and green jobs, as well as strengthening natural infrastructures and global resources.

COMPREHENSION

次の文を読み、本文の内容と合っていればT、そうでない場合はFを選択しましょう。

1. The air became cleaner than before the pandemic due to self-quarantine and less daily activity by humans.   [T / F]

2. It is clear that the pandemic's impact on the environment was huge.   [T / F]

3. Drops in fuel consumption and the price of oil can be seen as positive trends in the fossil fuel industry. [T / F]

4. A recovery of nature after the pandemic has not been seen all around the world. [T / F]

MAKE A SUMMARY

DL 106 ・ CD2-79

内容に合うように下線部に適切な語句や文を入れ、要約を完成させましょう。

　　　The global pandemic of COVID-19 has had some effects on the environment. [1]_____ improved and carbon emissions [2]_____ _____. Wildlife also changed. Some animals were seen in city areas and less traffic [3]_____ _____. However, according to environmental campaigners, not all effects brought on the environment by the pandemic were positive. In poor countries, the decrease in revenue toward conserving wildlife could result in increased [4]_____ _____. Nonetheless, there are a lot of things [5]_____ _____.

HAVE YOUR SAY

以下は "What can you do to save the environment?" という問いに対する、ある学生の回答です。ペアを組み、下線部を自分たちに置き換えて、配布された記入用紙に書いてみましょう（その後、クラスで発表してみましょう）。

> To save the environment, first I will buy a plastic bag for shopping and re-use it. I can also buy a reusable straw and carry it around with me when I go out. Car emissions are also bad for the environment so I will try to use public transportation such as buses and trains and ride my bicycle to go to nearby areas. These may seem small, but doing small things everyday will help us build a better future.

ご採用の先生方へ

本テキストには教授用資料に付録問題があり、それらは次に説明する CheckLink に対応しています（このテキスト自体には CheckLink 対応の問題はありませんのでご注意ください）。

CheckLink を使用しなくても問題は解けますが、授業活性化に役立つツールです。右ページをご参考いただき、ぜひご活用ください。

なお、付録の内容などの詳しい説明は、教授用資料にありますので、そちらもご参考いただけますと幸いです。

本書は CheckLink（チェックリンク）対応テキストです。

CheckLinkのアイコンが表示されている設問は、CheckLink に対応しています。

CheckLink を使用しなくても従来通りの授業ができますが、特色をご理解いただき、授業活性化のためにぜひご活用ください。

CheckLinkの特色について

　大掛かりで複雑な従来のe-learningシステムとは異なり、CheckLink のシステムは大きな特色として次の3点が挙げられます。

1. これまで行われてきた教科書を使った授業展開に大幅な変化を加えることなく、専門的な知識なしにデジタル学習環境を導入することができる。
2. PC教室やCALL教室といった最新の機器が導入された教室に限定されることなく、普通教室を使用した授業でもデジタル学習環境を導入することができる。
3. 授業中での使用に特化し、教師・学習者双方のモチベーション・集中力をアップさせ、授業自体を活性化することができる。

▶教科書を使用した授業に「デジタル学習環境」を導入できる

　本システムでは、学習者は教科書のCheckLinkのアイコンが表示されている設問にPCやスマートフォン、アプリからインターネットを通して解答します。そして教師は、授業中にリアルタイムで解答結果を把握し、正解率などに応じて有効な解説を行うことができるようになっています。教科書自体は従来と何ら変わりはありません。解答の手段としてCheckLinkを使用しない場合でも、従来通りの教科書として使用して授業を行うことも、もちろん可能です。

▶教室環境を選ばない

　従来の多機能なe-learning教材のように学習者側の画面に多くの機能を持たせることはせず、「解答する」ことに機能を特化しました。PCだけでなく、一部タブレット端末やスマートフォン、アプリからの解答も可能です。したがって、PC教室やCALL教室といった大掛かりな教室は必要としません。普通教室でもCheckLinkを用いた授業が可能です。教師はPCだけでなく、一部タブレット端末やスマートフォンからも解答結果の確認をすることができます。

▶授業を活性化するための支援システム

　本システムは予習や復習のツールとしてではなく、授業中に活用されることで真価を発揮する仕組みになっています。CheckLink というデジタル学習環境を通じ、教師と学習者双方が授業中に解答状況などの様々な情報を共有することで、学習者はやる気を持って解答し、教師は解答状況に応じて効果的な解説を行う、という好循環を生み出します。CheckLink は、普段の授業をより活力のあるものへと変えていきます。

　上記3つの大きな特色以外にも、掲示板などの授業中に活用できる機能を用意しています。従来通りの教科書としても使用はできますが、ぜひCheckLinkの機能をご理解いただき、普段の授業をより活性化されたものにしていくためにご活用ください。

CheckLink の使い方

CheckLink は、PC や一部のタブレット端末、スマートフォン、アプリを用いて、この教科書にある
 CheckLink のアイコン表示のある設問に解答するシステムです。
・初めて CheckLink を使う場合、以下の要領で**「学習者登録」**と**「教科書登録」**を行います。
・一度登録を済ませれば、あとは毎回**「ログイン画面」**から入るだけです。CheckLink を使う
　教科書が増えたときだけ、改めて**「教科書登録」**を行ってください。

CheckLink URL

https://checklink.kinsei-do.co.jp/student/

登録は **CheckLink 学習者用
アプリ**が便利です。ダウン
ロードはこちらから ▶ ▶ ▶

▶学習者登録 (PC /タブレット/スマートフォンの場合)

①上記 URL にアクセスすると、右のページが表示されます。学校名を入力し
　「ログイン画面へ」を選択してください。
　PC の場合は「**PC 用はこちら**」**を選択して** PC 用ページを表示します。同
　様に学校名を入力し「ログイン画面へ」を選択してください。
②ログイン画面が表示されたら「**初めての方はこちら**」を選択し
　「学習者登録画面」に入ります。

③自分の学籍番号、氏名、メールアドレス(学校
　のメールなど **PC メールを推奨**)を入力し、次
　に**任意のパスワード**を8桁以上20桁未満(半
　角英数字)で入力します。なお、学籍番号は
　パスワードとして使用することはできません。
④「パスワード確認」は、❸で入力したパスワー
　ドと同じものを入力します。
⑤最後に「登録」ボタンを選択して登録は完了
　です。次回からは、「ログイン画面」から学籍
　番号とパスワードを入力してログインしてく
　ださい。

▶教科書登録

①ログイン後、メニュー画面から「教科書登録」を選び（PCの場合はその後「新規登録」ボタンを選択）、「教科書登録」画面を開きます。

②教科書と受講する授業を登録します。
教科書の最終ページにある、**教科書固有番号**のシールをはがし、印字された**16桁の数字とアルファベット**を入力します。

③授業を担当される先生から連絡された**11桁の授業ID**を入力します。

④最後に「登録」ボタンを選択して登録は完了です。

⑤実際に使用する際は「教科書一覧」（PCの場合は「教科書選択画面」）の該当する教科書名を選択すると、「問題解答」の画面が表示されます。

▶問題解答

①問題は教科書を見ながら解答します。この教科書の  CheckLink のアイコン表示のある設問に解答できます。

②問題が表示されたら選択肢を選びます。

③表示されている問題に解答した後「解答」ボタンを選択すると解答が登録されます。

このシールをはがすと
CheckLink 利用のための
「**教科書固有番号**」が
記載されています。

一度はがすと元に戻すことは
できませんのでご注意下さい。

◀ ここからはがして下さい

4118 TARGET!
upper-intermediate   ◯ CheckLink ◦

本書には音声 CD（別売）があります

TARGET!　upper-intermediate
総合英語のターゲット演習【準上級】

2021 年 1 月 20 日　初版第 1 刷発行
2023 年 2 月 20 日　初版第 4 刷発行

著　者　　森　田　　彰
　　　　　飯　尾　牧　子
　　　　　橋　本　健　広
　　　　　角　田　麻　里
　　　　　佐　竹　麻　衣
　　　　　Taron Plaza

発行者　　福　岡　正　人
発行所　　株式会社　**金 星 堂**
（〒 101-0051）東京都千代田区神田神保町 3-21
Tel. (03) 3263-3828（営業部）
　　(03) 3263-3997（編集部）
Fax (03) 3263-0716
http://www.kinsei-do.co.jp

編集担当　長島吉成　　　　　　　　　Printed in Japan
印刷所・製本所／倉敷印刷株式会社

ISBN978-4-7647-4118-8　　C1082